MW00804010

# Theater, Drama, and Reading

# NCTE Editorial Board

Steven Bickmore

Catherine Compton-Lilly

Deborah Dean

Antero Garcia

Bruce McComiskey

Jennifer Ochoa

Staci M. Perryman-Clark

Anne Elrod Whitney

Vivian Yenika-Agbaw

Kurt Austin, Chair, ex officio

Emily Kirkpatrick, ex officio

# Theater, Drama, and Reading

## Transforming the Rehearsal Process into a Reading Process

Judith Freeman Garey
*Professor Emerita, Ventura College*

NATIONAL COUNCIL OF TEACHERS OF ENGLISH
340 N. NEIL ST., SUITE #104, CHAMPAIGN, ILLINOIS 61820
WWW.NCTE.ORG

"Oranges" from *New and Selected Poems* © 1995 by Gary Soto. Used with permission of Chronicle Books LLC, San Francisco. Visit ChronicleBooks.com.

"Thank You, M'am" from SHORT STORIES by Langston Hughes. Copyright © 1996 by Ramona Bass and Arnold Rampersad. Reprinted by permission of Hill and Wang, a division of Farrar, Straus and Giroux. Reprinted by permission of Harold Ober Associates. Copyright 1997 by the Langston Hughes Estate.

*Staff Editor:* Bonny Graham

*Manuscript Editor:* Tom Tiller

*Interior Design:* Jenny Jensen Greenleaf

*Cover Design:* Pat Mayer

*Cover Images:* Judith Freeman Garey

NCTE Stock Number: 53635; eStock Number: 53659
ISBN 978-0-8141-5363-5; eISBN 978-0-8141-5365-9

©2021 by the National Council of Teachers of English.

All rights reserved. No part of this publication may be reproduced or transmitted in any form or by any means, electronic or mechanical, including photocopy, or any information storage and retrieval system, without permission from the copyright holder. Printed in the United States of America.

It is the policy of NCTE in its journals and other publications to provide a forum for the open discussion of ideas concerning the content and the teaching of English and the language arts. Publicity accorded to any particular point of view does not imply endorsement by the Executive Committee, the Board of Directors, or the membership at large, except in announcements of policy, where such endorsement is clearly specified.

NCTE provides equal employment opportunity (EEO) to all staff members and applicants for employment without regard to race, color, religion, sex, national origin, age, physical, mental or perceived handicap/disability, sexual orientation including gender identity or expression, ancestry, genetic information, marital status, military status, unfavorable discharge from military service, pregnancy, citizenship status, personal appearance, matriculation or political affiliation, or any other protected status under applicable federal, state, and local laws.

Every effort has been made to provide current URLs and email addresses, but because of the rapidly changing nature of the web, some sites and addresses may no longer be accessible.

**Library of Congress Cataloging-in-Publication Data**
Names: Garey, Judith Freeman, 1949- author.
Title: Theater, drama, and reading : transforming the rehearsal process into a reading process / Judith Freeman Garey.
Description: Champaign, Illinois : National Council of Teachers of English, [2021] | Includes bibliographical references and index. | Summary: "Shows readers how to transform text from print to interaction by establishing a simple framework for how to read as an actor who builds characters' lives, a set designer who constructs context, and a director who generates action"—Provided by publisher.
Identifiers: LCCN 2021014578 (print) | LCCN 2021014579 (ebook) | ISBN 9780814153635 (Trade Paperback) | ISBN 9780814153659 (Adobe PDF)
Subjects: LCSH: Drama in education.
Classification: LCC PN3171 .G345 2021 (print) | LCC PN3171 (ebook) | DDC 371.3/99—dc23
LC record available at https://lccn.loc.gov/2021014578
LC ebook record available at https://lccn.loc.gov/2021014579

*For Christina*

# Contents

# Foreword

SHERIDAN BLAU, *Columbia University*

The riches of *Theater, Drama, and Reading: Transforming the Rehearsal Process into a Reading Process* will become quickly evident to any teacher who begins to thumb through its pages. I want to honor it as a contribution to the teaching of English by first setting it in its historical and pedagogical context. So let me begin with the somewhat dramatic, but hardly exaggerated, statement that the profession of English in America has been in need of Judy Garey's new book on theater, drama, and reading for roughly 130 years, at least since the 1890s, when English emerged from rhetoric and oratory to become a major subject in schools and colleges.

The need for and importance of Garey's book, from a historical perspective, resides in the curious fact that for most of the history of the teaching of English, the teaching of literature has not been conducted with any attention to the experience of literature as literature. That is to say, literary works in most colleges and secondary schools—most notably from about 1890 through World War II—were taught, studied, and valued in schools and colleges primarily for the instruction they could provide in subjects or discourses other than literature itself. Thus, literary texts were taught, or rather used, to teach grammar or for the examples they could provide of masterful rhetoric. They were also used as material for practice in oratory or for how they exemplified and advanced moral, civic, or religious values or provided lessons in cultural and political history. Most influentially (especially in universities), literary works were used for the study of philology—a discipline that examined the history of the English language and the related history of Anglo-Saxon folklore, along with the classical sources for more modern literary tropes and myths.

If we examine the history of literature itself, however, rather than the history of teaching it, we find that the most admired authors and critics in the Western literary tradition have consistently spoken of literature as a distinctive kind of discourse by virtue of the fact that it is not designed to serve purposes external to itself but is a discourse that comes into its own existence by being *experienced* by a reader. The learning that literature enables, therefore, was seen as similar to the learning that comes from living. Hence, Aristotle saw tragedies as psychologically therapeutic for auditors whose experience of a tragedy on the stage would bring about a catharsis in the discharge of feelings of pity and fear (46). Subsequently, the idea of literature as experience was confirmed by virtually every classical commentator on literature who quoted or rephrased Horace's dictum that the function of literature is to teach and delight or to teach through delight—the delight of a literary experience. The same idea was repeated and used by Sir Philip Sidney in his "Defense of Poetry" in 1580 to support his larger claim that poetry (by which he meant fiction) is a better teacher than philosophy or history precisely because the reader of literature learns through experience rather than through the abstract concepts of philosophy, and because poets (unlike historians) are free to construct imaginatively whatever experience would be most educative for readers (485–88). Yet, as in most enterprises represented by school subjects, the greatest wisdom about learning in the world outside of school has generally been ignored by pedants in favor of standards and traditions that valorize the role of teaching and marginalize learning in the teaching-learning relationship.

This pattern may also explain how it happened that both of the two most significant contributions in the history of literary studies to pedagogical thinking about literature sought to move the discourse of literature away from a discourse of information about literary texts and toward an experience of those texts: yet both seem to have devolved into teaching methodologies that eventually debased the learning theories they ostensibly derived from by promoting reading practices that substituted trivial observations or unfettered impressions in place of interpretations arising from thoughtful and deeply engaged experiences of a literary work. I am speaking of the two transformative theories of reading literature that emerged in the twentieth century and appeared, by some mystical coincidence, in books published in the same year of 1938. The first of these books (no longer used in any of its several editions except by literary historians), *Understanding Poetry* by Cleanth Brooks and Robert Penn Warren, introduced students and their teachers to what became known shortly thereafter as the principles of the New Criticism, a mode of reading that guided readers to experience a poem not as a historical, informational, or philosophical document, nor as a verbal structure that might be represented in a paraphrase, but, as Andrew Rejan convincingly demonstrates, an aesthetic experience structured by the formal properties of the poem. The other transformative book published in that same year was Louise Rosenblatt's classic and still widely read volume *Literature as Exploration*, introducing her transactional theory of reading literature, which emphasizes the reader's active role in constructing meaning through a direct encounter with a literary text, where the reader's individual experience of the text is constantly shaping and being reshaped by the text to produce what she refers to as a "warranted" interpretation. (Garey herself refers to Rosenblatt as a kind of theoretical precursor for some of her thinking about the rationale for her own pedagogical practice.)

Ironically, the book by Brooks and Warren that is now out of print and no longer read became widely used in college English classes and helped to launch the New Criticism as the dominant and almost undisputed theory for practice in the teaching of literature for roughly thirty years, from the late 1940s into the mid and late 1970s in colleges and universities, ultimately dominating the teaching of literature in secondary schools from the late 1960s to the end of the twentieth century and beyond. Interestingly, just as the New Criticism seemed to have exhausted its credibility among secondary English teachers, it was largely resuscitated in 2010 with the circulation and subsequent adoption of the Common Core State Standards in most American school districts. In the meantime, Rosenblatt's book, which continues to be studied and revered in the field of English education but is largely ignored in college and university English departments, has engendered a legacy of books and articles by two generations of her disciples who have tried to show how to apply and extend and even revise her theory for use in contemporary classrooms.

Unfortunately, however, in a historical progression that seems almost inevitable, the New Criticism as it came to be widely practiced in colleges and schools devolved into a perfunctory process of noting and analyzing technical features of a literary work and became what Robert Scholes called "a screen" between the student and the work of art (35). Transactional theory, in the meantime, continues to exert enormous influence among professionally well-informed scholars and teacher educators in the field of English education, but it seems to have achieved its greatest popularity among classroom teachers in the form of a theoretically reductive practice of "reader response" that appears to authorize any response a student reader might express without reference to the transactional model that requires students to take into account the details of the text that might force them to interrogate their response and reexamine and thereby reexperience their sense of the text and their understanding of the meaning of their experience. Rosenblatt's most accomplished disciples, in the meantime, have surely had a salutary influence on preservice and inservice English teachers, but the traditions of practices that favor teaching information about literature over the experience of literature have persisted in many secondary schools, especially in an era when those traditions are supported by an increasingly dominant culture of testing and high-stakes assessments.

Which brings us to Garey's book, a book that seems to me nearly bulletproof in its capacity to resist any effort to turn literary study more into an occasion for teaching than an opportunity for learning. Under her tactful direction, the literary text becomes an invitation to an aesthetic and theatrical experience—which is to say an engagement with life as that life is performed in accordance with language that can be considered, as it were, stage directions. Thus, to read a fictional text as it is envisioned in the theatrical rehearsal process is to enter into the fictional world of the text, feeling what characters feel, thinking their very thoughts, and inhabiting their constructed world. Nor does this process, as Garey enacts it, ignore such traditional academic matters as the apprehension of ideas, the tracking of inferences, or the analysis of motives, since all such considerations are a part of the theater artists' inquiry through the rehearsal process into how to play a character or understand the situation in which a character is placed. Hence, Garey's highly progressive method provides teachers and their students with an approach to reading that even manages to meet the Common Core State Standards and the standards of similar testing regimes, without sacrificing the inquiry-based and aesthetic orientation of her dramatic instruction.

Garey's method also goes beyond most other attempts I am aware of by expert teachers and former actors to use the rehearsal process as a model for learning. Unlike most efforts at dramatic teaching, she considers not only the actor's perspective, but also the director's and the designer's. The perspective of the designer, she points out, is especially crucial for interrogating and understanding the context for any scene or story, and the perception of the director, she explains, is fundamental to comprehending how action communicates a story's meaning.

Among the other unanticipated features of Garey's instructive book is her timely treatment of how to apply her rehearsal method in a class that is being conducted online. We may not have been waiting for that kind of assistance since the 1890s, but we have needed it since somewhere around the middle of March 2020.

Finally, it must be noted that Garey's book is arriving at about the same time that the National Council of Teachers of English (NCTE) has issued a position statement (Whitmore et al.) declaring that drama and drama-based pedagogies deserve an important place in English language arts classrooms. The NCTE statement presents the research evidence and theory, which it summarizes under the heading of "Key Message":

Research shows that learners' emotions and bodies (particularly in movement) are primary vehicles for meaning making in literacy classrooms (Caldas, 2018; Chisholm & Whitmore, 2018; Edmiston, 2014; Landay & Wootton, 2012; Roser, Martinez, et al., 2014). Research also indicates that access to multiple ways of knowing

(Harste, 2014; NCTE, 2005) supports learners' transmediation across sign systems (Siegel, 1995). Therefore, teachers should provide learners with opportunities to dramatize meanings in conjunction with literature and other texts.

Judy Garey's book turns the principles and theoretical arguments of that important policy statement into a discourse that is emotionally attuned, bodily oriented, practically organized, and dramatically represented in a manner that will effectively assist classroom teachers in knowing what to do and how to do it, in real time with real students for real learning.

## Works Cited

Aristotle. "Poetics." *The Critical Tradition: Classic Texts and Contemporary Trends*. 2nd ed., edited by David H. Richter, Bedford Books, 1998.

Brooks, Cleanth, and Warren, Robert Penn. *Understanding Poetry: An Anthology for College Students*. Henry Holt & Company, 1938.

Rejan, Andrew. "Reconciling Rosenblatt and the New Critics: The Quest for an 'Experienced Understanding' of Literature." *English Education*, vol. 50, no. 1, 2017, pp. 10–41.

Rosenblatt, Louise. *Literature as Exploration*. Appleton-Century, 1938.

Scholes, Robert. "Mission impossible." *English Journal*, vol. 88, no. 1, 1999, pp. 28–35.

Sidney, Sir Philip. "The Defense of Poetry." *The Norton Anthology of English Literature*. Vol. 1, 6th ed., edited by M. H. Abrams, W. W. Norton, 1993.

Whitmore, Kathryn F., et al. "Drama-Based Literacies." *Position Statements*. National Council of Teachers of English, 5 Aug. 2020, https://ncte.org/statement/drama-based-literacies/.

# Acknowledgments

This book developed out of many years of theatrical rehearsal, classroom practice, educational research, and a confluence of ideas. Many thanks to Barbara Cambridge, Pat Hutchings, Mary Huber, and Lee Shulman of the Carnegie Academy; Sheridan Blau, Carol Dixon, and Judith Green of the University of California, Santa Barbara; and Edith Conn and Ola Washington of Ventura College for your support of this work in its early stages.

With greatest appreciation to my husband, Tom Garey, for your support and technical expertise, Steve Dolainski for your advice and writing savvy, Rebecca Miller and Cathi Speake for access to your language arts classrooms, Cie Gumucio for your perceptive writing, Ben Crop and Scott Garey for your advice on virtual programs, Sheridan Blau and Tim Dewar for your continuing mentorship, and the fellows of the South Coast Writing Project for your ongoing encouragement of this work. Additional thanks to the NCTE field reviewers and to NCTE editors Kurt Austin, Bonny Graham, and Tom Tiller for your guidance in shaping this work.

My sincere gratitude to the many talented and dedicated theater artists with whom I have collaborated—actors, designers, directors, and production staff—who work tirelessly to bring the meaning of literature to life on the stage, and who have inspired me to share that process in this book for language arts teachers.

# Preface

## *Rethinking the Dynamics of Reading*

As a child, I found reading dull and passive. Although most of my family seemed to like this lifeless activity, to me it was a chore, something I had to do for school. Reading was boring. Reading was decoding words. Reading was just sitting there; you didn't *do* anything. I especially remember my mother sitting in a chair reading for what seemed like hours. How could she just sit there for so long without *doing* anything? To me, reading was tedious and little more than a waste of time.

It wasn't until I became a theater major in college that I discovered the magic of reading. I came to realize that reading was not about decoding words; nor was it boring or just sitting there. It was an extraordinary and imaginative journey. Moreover, it was the key to making text *visible*. As I participated in the rehearsal process for countless stage productions as a college student, I realized that we always started with reading. Every rehearsal process began with the entire cast and crew gathered around a table reading the script aloud. This reading was not about decoding words, however; it was about *interacting* with them and *transforming* them into a world of people, space, sound, and action for the stage.

This was a very different approach to reading, and it completely changed the way I connected with and understood literature. I realized that reading lays the foundation for stage productions and constitutes the first step in an interactive process to convert words into environment, action, and human behavior that make text perceptible for an audience. In this process, set designers, lighting designers, and costume designers envision and construct the visual elements of the literature, while directors and performers develop characters and generate the story's action. This process synthesizes the writer's words and the artists' insights into a living stage production. I realized that if people routinely went through this entire process it would take months to read a book, but I also recognized a strong takeaway for readers: whether one is reading to build a stage production or reading to understand a class assignment, the result is much richer when the reader interacts with the text.

Of course, this view of reading is not new. As early as 1938, in *Literature as Exploration*, Louise Rosenblatt advocated for the reader as an active agent in the reading process. Rosenblatt perceived the act of reading as involving reciprocal influence between reader and text in the making of meaning (xvi). From this perspective, reading is a process, a two-way relationship between the reader and the text, and a discovery of meaning through the transaction between the two as text and reader continually interact with each other. The importance of the reader as an active participant in the reading process was perfectly encapsulated by Rosenblatt: "A novel or a poem or a play remains merely ink spots on paper until a reader transforms them into a set of meaningful symbols" (24). Acknowledging that reading is a transaction between the reader and the text, readers can construct meaning as theater artists do—by building on the author's words with their own ideas.

After college, I went on to become a theater teacher and stage director and spent many years bringing texts to life on the stage. For every production, I began with reading. Reading established the foundation on which I built the lives of characters, envisioned the context in which they lived, and generated the action that told their story. Reading was no longer about decoding words; rather, each text was an adventure waiting to be unpacked. Now I couldn't wait to read, because I saw text as a distilled version of the human experience waiting for me to interact with it and give it life.

I realized, however, that for many of my students, texts never came to life as they did for me; they couldn't "see" what they were reading (Wilhelm, *You Gotta BE the Book* xii), and, consequently, the reading process never progressed beyond the decoding stage. *Theater, Drama, and Reading: Transforming the Rehearsal Process into a Reading Process* focuses on those students and delivers a specific set of strategies to help them transform reading into an interactive process of making text visible, concrete, and meaningful.

Using the world of theatrical practice as a model, the book illustrates how the theater artists' process of visualizing and activating text for the stage can be adapted into a specific set of reading strategies that all readers can learn. This approach challenges students to read responsively and imaginatively, uncovering evidence and asking questions of the text as they read, thus transforming reading into an interactive journey instead of a passive struggle to answer questions for a test. Concentrating on the work of three types of theater artists—actor, designer, and director—*Theater, Drama, and Reading* demonstrates how the rehearsal strategies of each artist can give readers a way to see and experience what they read.

Before beginning this approach to reading, however, teachers and students must accept the fact that reading, like any other meaningful pursuit, is a *process*: a series of steps taken to achieve a successful result. Generally, students will acknowledge that figuring out a math problem involves several attempts before arriving at the right answer, and most students will even accept that writing requires editing, rewriting, and numerous drafts before a successful product is achieved. Somewhere along the line, however, reading seems to have missed the boat. Most students still regard it as "once and done" and expect that if there's any significance to it, the teacher will fill it in.

Theater artists view text from a very different perspective. They know that the words on the page are not all that is there; a text contains layers of meaning that can never be fully captured in words alone. They see text not as the end product but as a *foundation to build on*. They don't *do* reading; they *use* reading as a discovery process, thus repositioning it from decoding words to transforming them into concrete, imaginative, and meaningful reality. This type of reading is both an inquiry process and a participatory one; although the text provides information, its meaning is something that theater artists know they must construct. Actors, designers, and directors each work toward specific goals when they read. Actors read to build characters' lives, designers read to construct context, and directors read to generate action. Approaching text through the lens of each of these theater artists will provide English language arts students with specific steps to follow and goals to achieve as they read. Just as theater artists follow a series of steps to transform written text into tangible stage productions, students will learn to implement a similar series of steps to make printed words visible and give them meaning.

In addition to creating an intersection between the rehearsal process and the reading process, this book will familiarize teachers and students with learning strategies that use drama—an active and engaging learning process. It does not mean students will be acting in a play, or directing one, or designing a set. It does mean they will be engaging in a type of learning that is dynamic, active, and participatory, and this is where the book begins.

# Introduction

## *Connecting with Drama*

Although the words *drama* and *theater* are often used interchangeably, they come from separate etymological roots, which can help us understand how they are different. The word *theater* comes from the Greek *theatron*, which means "seeing place," whereas the word *drama* is derived from the Greek *dran,* which means "to do." We can think of theater, therefore, as "that which is seen," and of drama as "that which is done."

If theater is "that which is seen," then it requires an audience, and in its simplest form it is created in the unique transaction between performer and audience as both participate in a shared experience. Moreover, "that which is seen" is presented to illuminate an audience. A theatrical production team begins with a written text, then shapes and focuses it into a production through a rehearsal process that makes it visible and meaningful for an audience.

In educational environments, drama is generally regarded as theater—a discipline or field centering on the study of dramatic literature and its production elements, including the integration of these elements into stage productions prepared for an audience. Middle schools and high schools often employ drama teachers, and colleges maintain drama departments with faculty who teach the crafts of theater and work with students to create theatrical productions for an audience. Educational drama programs typically focus their work on creating a product for an audience, thus centering what they do as theater, or "that which is seen."

However, drama can also be viewed through a different lens. If we view it as "that which is done" and consider it as independent from "that which is seen," then it can be thought of as the *discovery process* that develops and creates the theatrical presentation. In this view, drama is not the finished product for the audience but the generative process that *makes* the text visible and facilitates the understanding of it.

As a stage director, I have always been aware of how effectively drama facilitates learning, and specifically how the rehearsal process consists of strategies that unpack the meaning of text. Over the years, I often marveled at how thoroughly my community college students grasped the meaning of a piece of literature when they participated in creating a stage production of it. They hadn't "studied" the text as they might have in an English class, but because they had participated in the rehearsal process, their comprehension of the text was profound.

How was this possible? What had they done in the rehearsal process to illuminate the text? What I realized was that they had not *studied* the text—they had *inhabited* it, constructing meaning at the intersection between written text and lived experience. They knew the meaning of the dialogue because they had used the words to achieve their characters' objectives; they understood the era in which the play was set because they had embodied its style, mannerisms, and customs; and they realized how the sequence of actions in the story built from the inciting incident through the rising action, the climax, and the denouement because they had experienced it. Through rehearsal, they had participated in a discovery process in which they were creative agents, using the text as a foundation on which to create meaning. Recognizing how comprehensively the rehearsal process had facilitated their learning, I realized that in the same way theater practitioners use a rehearsal process to transform text into meaning for an audience, students could apply a similar process to reading in order to transform text into meaning for themselves.

## Drama and Language Arts

As a classroom practice, drama has been applied to the language arts curriculum in many ways and has been given a variety of descriptors by practitioners, including *process drama* (O'Neill, *Drama Worlds*), *drama pedagogy* (Edmiston), and *action strategies* (Wilhelm, *Deepening Comprehension*), to name just a few. This application of drama refers not to creating a presentation for an audience but to using or applying drama strategies in the classroom to help learners strengthen affective skills and translate abstract text into concrete and visible reality. It includes activities such as role-playing, physically enacting stories, portraying characters from history or literature, creating tableaux or still images to symbolize ambiguous concepts or characters, answering questions or approaching writing as characters, and numerous other active and engaging strategies for teaching and learning. By establishing a learning environment of meaning construction rather than one of information reception, classroom drama generates an approach to learning that involves intellect, physicality, empathy, and imagination. As a result, it guides students to see the real world with more clarity in light of what is revealed through the imagined one (Wagner, *Dorothy Heathcote*

227). In the same way that a theatrical performance enlightens its audience, participation in drama informs the students who participate in it.

John Dewey, a founder of the progressive education movement in America, articulated many of the underlying principles that support drama as pedagogy. Dewey argued that active and social engagement is essential to the learning process and that a child's development grows naturally out of meaningful educational experiences. Dewey expressed the importance of interaction for learning in his influential publication *Experience and Education* (41), which also emphasized the role of the educator in shaping education so that learners can derive meaning from the learning experience (35).

However, it was Dorothy Heathcote, a British professor of drama in education, who built a solid foundation for drama as a learning strategy. Heathcote emphasized that drama for learning is oriented not toward an audience but toward the participants, thus creating a generative activity and providing a way to make the implicit explicit (Wagner, *Dorothy Heathcote* 147). One example is her "mantle of the expert" approach to teaching and learning, which grants students the mantle or responsibility of an expert in a learning situation. By positioning students as "servicers" of knowledge rather than "receivers" of it (Heathcote and Bolton 32), Heathcote used the classroom to construct an imaginary enterprise in which learners *apply* knowledge to accomplish a goal. Central to this strategy is the notion of the "teacher-in-role" (Wagner, *Educational Drama* 227)—that is, the practice of the teacher participating along with students within the circumstances of the imaginary enterprise as a mentor or coach to help them apply information and accomplish their goals. Using this strategy effectively, as Heathcote did, involves the teacher's assuming a role to develop and heighten student involvement, yet coming out of it when it is necessary to achieve distance and objectivity (Wagner, *Dorothy Heathcote* 128).

Heathcote illustrated both the mantle of the expert and the teacher-in-role strategies through her classroom practice. For instance, following a study of medieval monasteries, students "became" monks, Heathcote "became" the abbot, and together their task was to explain to those in another community how to establish a monastery (Heathcote and Bolton 45). Thus, instead of simply receiving information, they were framed as responsible individuals who engaged with knowledge, treated it as evidence and source material, and used it to accomplish a goal. By asking students to assume the responsibility for both discovering and applying knowledge, this approach takes an active and purposeful view of learning in which knowledge is not merely taken in but operated on (Heathcote and Bolton 32).

This learning strategy, a robust example of Vygotsky's concept of the "zone of proximal development" (84), demonstrates how the social dimension of learning and the presence of an empowering adult (in this case, the teacher-in-role) creates an environment within which learners can reach beyond their current capacity toward continued development (86). This dynamic way of applying drama to the learning process is woven throughout the content of this book in the strategies of reading as an actor, reading as a designer, reading as a director, and reading collaboratively, thus demonstrating anew the distinction between memorizing isolated facts and transforming them into meaning.

The work done by Heathcote has been extended by others in the field of language arts. Educator James Moffett, who articulated the relationship between drama and English in *Teaching the Universe of Discourse,* argued that drama and speech are not peripheral but central to a language curriculum (60). Advocating for the value of dramatic enactment to link words with actions and motives, Moffett defined drama as a way to help readers understand and perceive action in a text (63). Further emphasizing drama as an important part of the teaching of language arts, Moffett and Betty Jane Wagner's *Student-Centered Language Arts and Reading K–13* built a compelling argument for the use of drama in the learning process by illustrating how physical action creates concrete images for written language (42).

Heathcote's work is also drawn on extensively in *"You Gotta BE the Book"* by Jeffrey Wilhelm and *Imagining to Learn: Inquiry, Ethics, and Integration through Drama* by Wilhelm and Brian Edmiston, which address drama in terms of curricular design and classroom research. In addition to providing well-defined examples of her mantle of the expert approach and the use of teacher-in-role, these works cite Vygotsky as well as Jerome Bruner and Howard Gardner to support using drama as a pedagogical tool. Finally, Wilhelm's *Deepening Comprehension with Action Strategies* contributes a significant treatment of methods for language arts teachers interested in using drama in ways that engage students with text.

Additional publications in the field have associated drama as a learning strategy with the important workplace skills of creativity, collaboration, and teamwork; with teaching to multiple intelligences; and with the significance of arts integration into language arts classrooms to support literacy development. Moreover, in 2020, the National Council of Teachers of English (Whitmore et al.) issued a position statement across the categories of curriculum, instruction, and literacy to emphasize contemporary research and practice regarding the multimodal nature of literacies and to call on teachers to engage learners in composing, reading, and interrogating texts through drama-based literacies.

# Drama and the Common Core State Standards

The Common Core State Standards (CCSS) for English Language Arts (ELA) define broad literacy goals for students as stated in the College and Career Readiness Anchor (CCRA) Standards in Reading (R), Writing (W), Speaking and Listening (SL), and Language (L). These acronyms are used later in the book when Common Core standards are listed as they apply to various reading strategies. The Anchor Standards form the backbone of the ELA and literacy requirements by articulating core knowledge and skills that students should acquire and master in English language arts classrooms. The standards are further subdivided by grade levels that specifically define what students should understand and be able to do by the end of each grade.

Most of today's students are expected to meet the Common Core State Standards for English Language Arts. These standards represent a paradigm shift (Wilhelm, *Deepening Comprehension* 6) toward instruction that focuses on critical thinking, analysis, reasoning, and problem-solving skills to prepare students for success in college, career, and life. The standards stress reading and writing based on careful analysis of textual evidence and challenge students not just to read text but also to comprehend context and grasp how concepts relate to each other. Waiting for the teacher to supply meaning for a text will no longer suffice when students move on to college or into careers where they must read and comprehend increasingly complex texts independently. If we want students to read closely, effectively, and self-sufficiently, then we need to give them strategies for interacting with text instead of colliding with it and for gravitating toward reading rather than maintaining a distance from it.

*Theater, Drama, and Reading* offers teachers and students an interactive approach to achieving the Common Core State Standards for English Language Arts, not only in reading but also in writing, speaking, listening, and language. Section I of the book introduces you to specific strategies for teaching students to read as actors, designers, and directors. Section II then guides you step by step through classroom application of these reading strategies with two mentor texts, and Section III provides additional drama strategies for engaging students with text. Using role-playing and Dorothy Heathcote's mantle of the expert approach to learning, students will reposition themselves from *receivers* of text to *servicers* of it, reading with specific tasks to accomplish and goals to achieve in order to make text visible and meaningful. They will learn to read texts multiple times for multiple purposes, deepening their understanding each time they read, and they will be challenged and asked questions that push them to refer back to what they've read, closely and attentively analyzing text in a way that will help them understand it. Drawing perceptive inferences from textual evidence, they will learn to analyze word choice; evaluate how complex ideas develop throughout a text; and understand the relationship between characters, context, and action. Meanwhile, teachers will participate in role, coaching students through the process from within it and guiding them toward achievement of the Common Core State Standards for English Language Arts.

These reading strategies can be applied to any type of literature and can be implemented individually or collectively, in whole or in part, in a short amount of time or over a longer interval. As you read through each process, think of how you can adapt the strategies to your students and the literature you use in your curriculum to help your students achieve the ELA Common Core standards. These strategies use drama to shift the focus of reading from information reception to knowledge construction and give students a way to interact with text, think beyond words on the page, and transform text from abstract concepts into concrete representations. By making students responsible for understanding not only the words on the page but also what lies beneath and around them, the strategies challenge them to use inquiry and analysis as a foundation for reading and give them a way to transform words from print to interaction as they read.

Theater artists work toward the goal of converting text into stage productions. ELA students can learn to apply many of the same strategies to transform text into meaning, thus refocusing reading to the inquiry, analysis, and problem-solving skills they need in order to meet the Common Core State Standards and become successful and self-sufficient readers.

## Drama in an Online Environment

In a changing world, you may find yourself in a new and different educational realm where many things you have taken for granted—for instance, brick-and-mortar classrooms, collaborative communities of learners, and close contact with your students—have also changed. You may be teaching completely online, synchronously or asynchronously or both, and your time in a physical classroom may be a transformed experience. What you once did in your classroom, you can't do any more. Or perhaps it's not that things can't be done, but that they will need to be accomplished in a different way.

Drama, by its very nature, is a face-to-face activity. Its history in the classroom has always taken the form of a classroom experience and a social interaction. If you find you are no longer in a physical classroom, can you still use drama?

Absolutely.

Remember, drama as we have defined it is not the finished product for the audience but the generative process that makes text visible and facilitates understanding of it. I invite you to think of drama not as a performative endeavor but as a constructive and highly effective approach to learning and reading comprehension. Yes, it is a teaching and learning method with roots in the conventional classroom experience, but Dewey's advocacy for interaction in the learning experience and Dorothy Heathcote's mantle of the expert approach—not only gathering information but also applying it—can certainly transfer to a remote environment. What matters is not so much the mode of instruction, but the ability to implement the core principles of these reading strategies: reading interactively; reading in role; applying information to achieve goals; and drawing intelligent, imaginative conclusions from textual evidence by building characters' lives, constructing context, and generating action.

Online learning platforms and applications give you the capacity to facilitate interaction with an entire class or have students work in small groups. Students can also share documents, edit each other's work, create graphics, and communicate across great distances, working both synchronously and asynchronously. Therefore, while descriptions of classroom application in this book are taken from physical classroom experience, all of the reading strategies can be adapted to remote learning.

At the end of each classroom application chapter, I include suggestions for using the strategies in a virtual environment. Please feel free to use these suggestions as is or adapt them to your specific circumstances. Think creatively about how you can apply or modify any of these reading strategies to the learning environment in which you find yourself. By bringing students together to think imaginatively, collaborate, and solve problems, drama offers you a powerful approach to learning and building community in any classroom environment.

# Reading as a Theater Artist

Theater artists read differently. Reading to transform words and ideas into performance, they regard text as a gateway into a story's characters, context, and action. More specifically, actors read to build characters' lives, designers read to construct context, and directors read to generate action. To reach these goals, each artist follows a series of specific steps.

# Reading as an Actor

*Building Characters' Lives*

Actors read and transform written text through a generative process by using a series of steps designed to create, build, and develop a story's characters. Although fictional characters are conceived by the writer, it is the actor's responsibility to give their personalities and individual behaviors a concrete form. Actors undergo rigorous training to learn this craft. They study movement, voice, and script analysis and continually practice their skills through rehearsal and performance. We will focus here on how actors read and use text to build characters' lives. When actors read, they know they have responsibilities and goals to achieve. Regarding text as source material, they read and reread, building on what they find in the text to reach their goal of bringing characters to life.

Reading is an essential component of the actor's rehearsal process—typically, a six- to eight-week developmental endeavor for every production. The rehearsal process begins with a collaborative oral reading and continues through many weeks of exploring the text to learn characters' lines; create the story's action; and discover the implications, insinuations, and subtexts that help give both the words and actions their meaning. As actors read and reread the text, they study both the denotations and the connotations of the writer's words, searching for nuances that define each character's personality and behavior. They deconstruct, paraphrase, and reconstruct language to understand why the writer has chosen specific words, and they build on the text to construct elements of a character's life not specified by the writer, thus giving characters continuity and depth. Finally, they compare choices, consider options, and ultimately choose specific vocal, physical, cognitive, and affective qualities that will express each character's unique personality and the writer's meaning to the audience. By the end of the rehearsal process, each actor has read the text and analyzed specific parts of it many times over. If actors stopped the reading process after the initial read-through, they would never achieve the depth of understanding needed to express the significance of the characters and the story to an audience.

While there is no need for ELA students to engage in the demanding training and rehearsal methods of an actor, specific steps of the actor's process can help them read with greater depth. In this discussion, the actor's rehearsal process is condensed into three steps that students can follow to improve their grasp of literary characters, their relationships, and the continuity of their lives:

**Steps of Reading as an Actor**

1. Search for and record evidence of character from the text.

2. Generate character biographies and relationships.

3. Fill in any time gaps in the story line.

I always provide actors with a worklist detailing their specific tasks and reading goals. You will see examples of the actor's worklist in action in Section II, Application in the Classroom.

## Step 1: Search for and Record Evidence of Character from the Text

Actors begin with a focused reading of the text to uncover all of the facts that the writer has supplied about the characters; they are searching for specifics such as age, place of birth, physical characteristics, family background, education, language use, and significant events that have shaped characters' lives. Insight into characters' lives and personalities may be embedded in the text in a multitude of ways: how they are described, what they say in conversation, what other characters say about them, how they behave in various situations, and the ways in which they interact with other characters.

Similarly, as ELA students read to find character evidence, they must take notes to record what they discover. They can write directly on the text, record notes on a separate paper or a screen, or use worksheets to record everything the writer has supplied regarding characters' backgrounds, relationships, and behaviors. Worksheets for the actor are provided in the appendix.

---

**Applicable Common Core Goals**

**CCSS.ELA-Literacy. CCRA.R.1**

Read closely to determine what the text says explicitly and to make logical inferences from it; cite specific textual evidence when writing or speaking to support conclusions drawn from the text.

---

CCSS.ELA-Literacy. CCRA.R.6

Assess how point of view or purpose shapes the content and style of a text.

## Step 2: Generate Character Biographies and Relationships

Actors then *apply* what they have discovered in the text, make inferences, and draw conclusions to create a *biography* of each character and develop the character's *relationships*. Students can do the same, which engages them in developing and using more sophisticated reading and thinking skills.

A character biography gives a complete account of a character's life. It should begin with the character's date and place of birth and include all events that have shaped the character into the person found in the story. Remind students that they can readily accomplish this task because they can certainly write their own autobiography. Just as students can document their own lives from birth through the significant events that have shaped them into the people they are today, they can generate a similar biography for a literary character by finding analogous details in the text and supplementing that information through imaginative extrapolation based on textual evidence.

In addition to creating individual characters' biographies, students must investigate the text to develop the relationships *between* the characters. What has occurred in the past to create the character relationships as defined by the writer? Have certain characters known each other for a long period of time, or have they just met? What relationships are evident, and what is being concealed? How do characters interact with each other one on one, how do they interact in a group, and why do certain interactions occur? If, for instance, a character says, "I have hated so-and-so since the incident on the boat," then students must determine what the incident was, when it happened, what occurred between the characters, and what lasting effects it produced. As they engage in this process, students will discover, as actors do, that not all details of characters' lives are specified by the writer. When actors can't find information within the text, they must make inferences from the text to plausibly complete the specifics of characters' relationships. Students can do the same. While they must base all conclusions on evidence found in the text, this process gives them the opportunity to build on that evidence with their own imagination.

Creating characters' biographies and developing their relationships not only gives readers specific goals to work toward; it also turns them into detectives as they search the text for clues and piece together answers. This process of finding information and building on it asks readers to discover not only the *what* of characters' lives but also the *where, when,* and *why.* Through this process, reading shifts to inquiry and analysis as readers ask questions and draw conclusions based on evidence from the text. This process is the reason that two actors' portrayal of the same character will never be exactly the same. Each actor started with the same text but supplements the fictional life of the character with individual imaginative, yet logical, conclusions based on the text.

As students engage in the same process—inferring from the text and drawing logical conclusions about events in characters' lives—they build reading and thinking skills. If a story takes place in 1945 and a character is twenty years old, the reader can conclude that the character was born in 1925 and must then build the character's formative years based on events and conditions in that time frame. As readers engage in this process, they must search the text judiciously and think events through to reasonable conclusions. Aside from giving students motivation for in-depth reading, this process creates wonderful discussion opportunities about choices that students make and why. Different students, like different actors, will come to different conclusions, and allowing them to compare their results will generate thought-provoking discussion of characters' lives as readers justify their choices.

This step of the actor's process also creates a significant writing opportunity. Students can develop character biographies and describe characters' relationships in quick-writes or more comprehensive writing assignments.

---

**Applicable Common Core Goals**

**CCSS.ELA-Literacy. CCRA.R.1**

Read closely to determine what the text says explicitly and to make logical inferences from it; cite specific textual evidence when writing or speaking to support conclusions drawn from the text.

**CCSS.ELA-Literacy. CCRA.R.2**

Determine central ideas or themes of a text and analyze their development; summarize the key supporting details and ideas.

**CCSS.ELA-Literacy. CCRA.R.3**

Analyze how and why individuals, events, or ideas develop and interact over the course of a text.

**CCSS.ELA-Literacy. CCRA.R.4**

Interpret words and phrases as they are used in a text, including determin-

---

ing technical, connotative, and figurative meanings, and analyze how specific word choices shape meaning or tone.

**CCSA.ELA-Literacy. CCRA.W.1**

Write arguments to support claims in an analysis of substantive topics or texts using valid reasoning and relevant and sufficient evidence.

**CCSS.ELA-Literacy. CCRA.W.3**

Write narratives to develop real or imagined experiences or events using effective technique, well-chosen details, and well-structured event sequences.

## Step 3: Fill in Any Time Gaps in the Story Line

The third step in the actor's process gives students the opportunity to delve further into the text and find another layer of meaning by filling in gaps in the story line. Writers often skip over periods of time as they tell a story, and it is important for readers to identify what occurs during this "lost time" in order to maintain a sense of continuity in characters' lives. When I work with actors, we improvise physically and verbally to create action and dialogue that bridge any time gaps left by the writer. Students can accomplish this same step through discussion or writing. For example, if Chapter 2 of a story begins six weeks after Chapter 1 ends, students must think through what happened during that interval. What activities were characters involved in during the missing time? Did relationships between characters change? How are the characters different at the beginning of Chapter 2 than they were at the end of Chapter 1, and what happened to precipitate the change? Students can also hypothesize about what occurs before a story begins and after it ends—once again drawing conclusions based on textual evidence, thus engaging with the text at a deeper level to find answers to new questions.

### Applicable Common Core Goals

**CCSS.ELA-Literacy. CCRA.R.1**

Read closely to determine what the text says explicitly and to make logical inferences from it; cite specific textual evidence when writing or speaking to support conclusions drawn from the text.

**CCSS.ELA-Literacy. CCRA.R.3**

Analyze how and why individuals, events, or ideas develop and interact over the course of a text.

**CCSS.ELA-Literacy. CCRA.R.5**

Analyze the structure of texts, including how specific sentences, paragraphs, and larger portions of the text (e.g., a section, chapter, scene, or stanza) relate to each other and the whole.

**CCSA.ELA-Literacy. CCRA.W.1**

Write arguments to support claims in an analysis of substantive topics or texts using valid reasoning and relevant and sufficient evidence.

**CCSS.ELA-Literacy. CCRA.W.3**

Write narratives to develop real or imagined experiences or events using effective technique, well-chosen details, and well-structured event sequences.

Each step of the actor's process—searching for and recording evidence of character from the text, generating character biographies and relationships, and filling in time gaps in the story line—asks readers to examine characters at a deeper level and look at them from a different perspective. In this way, the actor's process engages students with high-level cognitive questions, thereby helping them develop more meaningful and multilayered insight into characters.

# Reading as a Designer

## *Constructing Context*

Designers read and transform text with a lens different from the one used by actors. The reading process of a designer focuses not on character but on discovering and creating a story's context, or the conditions within which the story occurs. Theatrical designers create a stage production's settings, lighting, costumes, makeup, sound design, and special effects. Although the work of all of these designers is essential to a stage production, we focus here on the set designer's process of creating a story's physical environment, which is especially beneficial in helping students "see" what they are reading.

Like actors, set designers read a text multiple times and have specific goals to achieve. Each time they read, set designers investigate the text at a deeper level to find specific details. The designer's first reading of the text is geared toward acquiring a literal understanding of what the story is about, why it is being told, and who the characters are. Next, the set designer analyzes the text more closely to gather practical information about the context by asking questions. Does the story take place in one environment, or are there multiple locations? If there are multiple settings, how do characters move from one location to another? Do various locations need to be seen at the same time or separately? Does the action occur indoors, outdoors, or both? What is the time period, and how can its art and architecture be represented? Does the action occur in specific spaces—such as rooms, windows, doors, or stairways—and if so, how do they accommodate the story's action? What furniture and props are needed in the environment?

Once set designers have read to gain a literal understanding of the text and have discovered its practical requirements, they must delve even deeper to find any symbolic or metaphorical meanings and decide how to represent them in the environment as well. Again, set designers ask questions as they read. What does the language in the text imply? Is the context symbolic of anything in the characters' lives? Is the story told through the perspective of a specific character? If so, how can that fact be expressed? Should the walls be solid, or do characters think about something that can be seen behind them? Are there times when two locations must be seen simultaneously? If so, how can that be represented in a way that implies their shared meaning? Do certain shapes, textures, or colors suggest the story's significance? How can the context represent not only the substance of the story but also its meaning?

In this way, designers read and reread, analyze, and search for detail and nuance in the text, continually uncovering additional layers of meaning. At this point, the set designer's process intersects with that of the director, and the two artists must confer and come to consensus about how the context will accommodate the story's action and visually communicate its meaning. Any differences must be discussed and resolved so that the designer and the director are working toward the same goals for the audience. Following consultation with the director, the set designer visualizes the context and creates drawings of it. From there, a technical director generates more detailed working drawings, and a crew builds the environment so that it is practical, safe, and visually meaningful.

To train for their craft, set designers study detailed script analysis and must learn both mechanical and computer-assisted drawing. They study art, architecture, math, physics, and engineering to learn painting techniques, construction methods, and principles of structural integrity. They must also know and observe all relevant safety guidelines and practices.

As readers, ELA teachers and students do not need such rigorous training; nor do we envision and construct as detailed and comprehensive a context as a theatrical set designer would. Our reading task is to discover the practical requirements and metaphorical implications of the context and envision what the environment might look like in the classroom. We then create a simple representation of it to help us see the context of the literature we are studying. The designer's process can be condensed into the following three steps:

**Steps of Reading as a Designer**

1. Search for and record evidence of context from the text.

2. Visualize the context in the classroom.

3. Create a representation of the context in the classroom.

I also provide the designers with a worklist detailing their specific tasks and reading goals. You will see examples of the designer's worklist in action in Section II, Application in the Classroom.

## Step 1: Search for and Record Evidence of Context from the Text

Reading as a set designer and regarding the text as source material from which to obtain evidence of context, students must look for two categories of information: explicit evidence stated directly in the text and implicit information tucked into the writer's word choices. For instance, a room described as "cramped" paints a different picture from one labeled as "exposed"; similarly, a "well-worn, well-loved family heirloom" evokes a distinctly different impression than "a utilitarian chair fresh out of its packing box." Thus, reading as a set designer means searching the text for the explicit *what* of the environment; looking closely at the language to determine the implicit *why, when,* and *where*; and making inferences and drawing conclusions based on all of this textual evidence. As readers search the text in the manner of designers, they should generate a list of props needed in the environment. This list includes any furniture or household or environmental items that the characters need in order to accomplish the story's action. During this search, readers must record what they find by writing directly on the text, taking notes on a separate paper or a laptop, or using worksheets. Worksheets for the designer are included in the appendix.

---

**Applicable Common Core Goals**

**CCSS.ELA-Literacy. CCRA.R.1**

Read closely to determine what the text says explicitly and to make logical inferences from it; cite specific textual evidence when writing or speaking to support conclusions drawn from the text.

**CCSS.ELA-Literacy. CCRA.R.4**

Interpret words and phrases as they are used in a text, including determining technical, connotative, and figurative meanings, and analyze how specific word choices shape meaning or tone.

**CCSS.ELA-Literacy. CCRA.R.5**

Analyze the structure of texts, including how specific sentences, paragraphs, and larger portions of the text (e.g., a section, chapter, scene, or stanza) relate to each other and the whole.

---

## Step 2: Visualize the Context in the Classroom

Once designers know all of the physical requirements of the context, have gained a sense of how the context can express the meaning of the text, and have consulted with the director, they are ready to create the environment for a specific architectural stage and production.

For us as readers, the goal is to envision a representation of the textual environment in the classroom. Using the explicit and implicit information gathered from the text, students now look at the classroom space and use their imagination to visualize how it can be reconfigured to create the context of the story. Don't move any furniture at this point; simply envision and discuss the possibilities. What space or spaces does the story's environment need, and how can the classroom and its furniture be reconfigured to create that context? Ask students to look at the classroom with fresh eyes and think imaginatively about how it could be transformed. If you move furniture around, what can you create? Chairs, desks, tables, bookcases, and various classroom odds and ends can be used inventively to represent almost any location. For example, two chairs with a space between them can easily become a doorway, a door itself can be pantomimed, a rolling whiteboard can represent a wall, and three chairs lined up together can become a sofa. Take the time to talk about any symbolic meaning of the context as you envision it but accept the fact that you will probably not be able to integrate too much metaphorical meaning into the context in a limited classroom construction of it.

This step of the designer's process can be accomplished individually or in small groups. As students think around and beyond the written word and visualize the story's environment in the classroom, they can either draw sketches of what they envision or write a description of it.

---

**Applicable Common Core Goals**

**CCSS.ELA-Literacy. CCRA.R.1**

Read closely to determine what the text says explicitly and to make logical inferences from it; cite specific textual evidence when writing or speaking to support conclusions drawn from the text.

**CCSS.ELA-Literacy. CCRA.R.5**

Analyze the structure of texts, including how specific sentences, paragraphs, and larger portions of the text (e.g., a section, chapter, scene, or stanza) relate to each other and the whole.

**CCSS.ELA-Literacy. CCRA.R.7**

Integrate and evaluate content presented in diverse media and formats, including visually and quantitatively, as well as in words.

---

## Step 3: Create a Representation of the Context in the Classroom

In this step, you will actually move furniture and create a representation of the story's context. Do not be alarmed! Remember that for readers, this part of the designer's process—building the context into reality—is not an exercise in stage construction, interior design, or creating a finished product for an audience. Rather, the purpose is to create a simple, concrete representation of the story's context to help students see its environment and experience it in three dimensions. Keep the process uncomplicated and don't allow it to become stressful. Make it simple and doable and accept the fact that you will not be able to replicate, say, an authentic eighteenth-century drawing room in your classroom. The goal is to create a simple and concrete representation of the context that readers can see.

As they engage in this process, readers will need to verify that the environment they build includes all of the practical elements needed to accommodate the story's action. Students must read and reread the text as they build the environment to confirm that their creation and placement of doors, windows, furniture, and other objects will provide for the specific actions in the story. They also need to ask questions such as the following: Where should a window be if a character needs to see a specific action occurring outside? How does furniture need to be arranged in relation to a door so that a character can walk into a room undetected? Is sufficient space allowed for characters to accomplish actions that need to happen as they move from one location to another?

From their initial search for context information, students will have generated a list of props. You can either bring in the necessary props or ask students to provide them. Again, keep it simple. Everyday items such as dish towels, throw pillows, flowerpots, and books can be found in most people's homes; more unusual props can be simply constructed or represented with paper, scissors, tape, and a bit of imagination. Once the classroom has been reconfigured, invite readers to place the props where they belong in the environment. Finally, when building an environment in the classroom, always leave time at the end of the session to put the room back in order.

---

**Applicable Common Core Goals**

**CCSS.ELA-Literacy. CCRA.R.1**

Read closely to determine what the text says explicitly and to make logical

---

inferences from it; cite specific textual evidence when writing or speaking to support conclusions drawn from the text.

**CCSS.ELA-Literacy. CCRA.R.5**

Analyze the structure of texts, including how specific sentences, paragraphs, and larger portions of the text (e.g., a section, chapter, scene, or stanza) relate to each other and the whole.

**CCSS.ELA-Literacy. CCRA.R.7**

Integrate and evaluate content presented in diverse media and formats, including visually and quantitatively, as well as in words.

**CCSS.ELA-Literacy. CCRA.R.8**

Delineate and evaluate the argument and specific claims in a text, including the validity of the reasoning as well as the relevance and sufficiency of the evidence.

**CCSS.ELA-Literacy. CCRA.SL.1**

Prepare for and participate effectively in a range of conversations and collaborations with diverse partners, building on others' ideas and expressing their own clearly and persuasively.

The three steps of the designer's process—searching for and recording context information, envisioning the context, and building it into reality—focus students' reading on the specifics of a story's context. As they read and reread the text to find both the practical considerations and the metaphorical implications of the context, integrate their own ideas with those of the writer to envision what it looks like, and build the environment in the classroom, they increase their insight into both the story's context and its meaning.

# 3

# Reading as a Director

## *Generating Action*

Directors transform text with an imaginative and multidimensional lens in order to create an overarching vision for a production and synchronize its many components. The director coordinates the efforts of all designers and performers to ensure a unified whole by organizing collaboration, conducting rehearsals, generating the physical action of the story, coaching actors, mediating disagreements, solving problems, and continually managing all aspects of the production as it progresses. Therefore, a director's expertise includes knowledge of a wide variety of dramatic literature and methods of scene analysis, as well as a working knowledge of all aspects of theater production.

Here, we focus on the directorial task that is most beneficial to readers: generating the story's action. Directors read and reread with the goal of finding the action and interaction that communicate the events of the story and express its meaning. Reading as a director means discovering a story's sequence of actions, determining their causality, envisioning how they will be represented, and transforming them into concrete reality. Our task as readers will not be as comprehensive and complex as that of a stage director; we will focus on finding the physical and verbal actions in the text, visualizing them, and enacting them in the classroom. The director's process can be condensed into the following three steps:

**Steps of Reading as a Director**

1. Search for and record evidence of physical and verbal action from the text.
2. Conceptualize the physical and verbal action.
3. Transform the action into concrete reality.

As I do with actors and designers, I provide directors with a worklist detailing their specific tasks and reading goals. You will see examples of the director's worklist in Section II, Application in the Classroom.

## What Are Physical Action and Verbal Action?

Action is how characters in a story achieve their objectives and goals. Physical action is bodily movement to accomplish a task. If I am sitting in my living room and hear the doorbell, I get up, walk to the door, and open it. That is physical action. Verbal action, in contrast, is the use of *language* to accomplish a task. If I am too lazy to walk to the door, I might say, "Come in. The door's unlocked." That is verbal action—using language to accomplish the task. Physical action can be achieved in many ways. I might slowly approach the door if I am uncertain who is there, run to it if it is urgent, or crawl if I am injured. Verbal action can also be expressed in many ways, not only through the words themselves but also through the manner in which they are spoken. Volume, pitch, rate of speech, and even silence can greatly affect meaning. I might shout if the door is far away or use slower and clearer diction if the person at the door has a hearing loss, or even stay silent if I want to give the impression that no one is home. Both categories of action—physical and verbal—are used to express meaning.

## Step 1: Search for and Record Evidence of Physical and Verbal Action from the Text

A director's first reading of a text is geared toward gaining a basic idea of the story line, the characters, and the context. Rereading the text, the director then delves deeper to identify all specific references to physical and verbal action that tell the story and accomplish the characters' objectives. Who does what to whom and why? How does one event precipitate another? How does one character's action affect others? How does each event move the story forward and change it? What sequence of events makes the story different at the end than it was at the beginning? In other words, the director must search the text carefully to find both direct and implied references to physical and verbal actions and identify how those actions and interactions move the story from start to finish. The director then needs to look at the end of the story and trace the actions back to the beginning, ensuring that each action has been motivated by a preceding one. Searching the text for physical and verbal action as directors, students take notes either by writing directly onto the text, recording notes on a separate paper or a laptop, or using worksheets. Worksheets for the director are provided in the appendix.

**Applicable Common Core Goals**

**CCSS.ELA-Literacy. CCRA.R.1**

Read closely to determine what the text says explicitly and to make logical inferences from it; cite specific textual evidence when writing or speaking to support conclusions drawn from the text.

**CCSS.ELA-Literacy. CCRA.R.3**

Analyze how and why individuals, events, or ideas develop and interact over the course of a text.

**CCSS.ELA-Literacy. CCRA.R.4**

Interpret words and phrases as they are used in a text, including determining technical, connotative, and figurative meanings, and analyze how specific word choices shape meaning or tone.

**CCSS.ELA-Literacy. CCRA.R.5**

Analyze the structure of texts, including how specific sentences, paragraphs, and larger portions of the text (e.g., a section, chapter, scene, or stanza) relate to each other and the whole.

## Step 2: Conceptualize the Physical and Verbal Action

Once directors identify *what* happens in the story, they must engage their imagination to decide *how* it happens. They determine the action patterns by asking questions. Who is dominant in a specific relationship, and how is that dynamic expressed physically or through language? What causes characters to move closer to each other or put distance between them? Do some characters speak louder and more forcefully than others? Why? What is happening during a silence? How do the physical and verbal actions signify how a story builds and reaches its climax? Reading as a director means not only identifying the physical and verbal actions but also determining how those actions are carried out to express the story's meaning and structure, both literal and metaphorical.

Just as there is no single correct way to complete a character's biography or represent a story's context, there is no set way to generate a story's action. The written text is a constant, but the same story can be represented through action in multiple ways. This is why two productions of the same text will never be exactly the same on the stage. Each team of directors, designers, and actors has started with the same text but then combined their imaginative ideas with the text in a unique way.

To accomplish this step of conceptualizing action, directors need an environment in which to locate the action. They can write out a description of what they envision as the environment or draw pictures to represent it. This is where the director's process and that of the designer intersect. In Section II, Application in the Classroom, you will see how I integrate the processes of the director and the designer when they work collaboratively, as well as how I coach directors through envisioning and building an environment when they are working without a designer.

---

**Applicable Common Core Goals**

**CCSS.ELA-Literacy. CCRA.R.1**

Read closely to determine what the text says explicitly and to make logical inferences from it; cite specific textual evidence when writing or speaking to support conclusions drawn from the text.

**CCSS.ELA-Literacy. CCRA.R.4**

Interpret words and phrases as they are used in a text, including determining technical, connotative, and figurative meanings, and analyze how specific word choices shape meaning or tone.

**CCSS.ELA-Literacy. CCRA.R.8**

Delineate and evaluate the argument and specific claims in a text, including the validity of the reasoning as well as the relevance and sufficiency of the evidence.

**CCSS.ELA-Literacy. CCRA.W.1**

Write arguments to support claims in an analysis of substantive topics or texts using valid reasoning and relevant and sufficient evidence.

**CCCS.ELA-Literacy. CCRA.W.3**

Write narratives to develop real or imagined experiences or events using effective technique, well-chosen details, and well-structured event sequences.

---

## Step 3: Transform the Action into Concrete Reality

Before the action of a story can be converted into concrete reality, the environment to accommodate it must be built. Referring back to the written descriptions or drawings they have created, students can rearrange the classroom to represent the environment. Keep this process simple and remember that its purpose is not to achieve an artistic masterpiece but to provide an accurate and practical environment for the story's action (see Chapter 2, "Reading as a Designer").

Once you have constructed the environment and are ready to create the action in the classroom, the director's process intersects with the actor's process. Select a group of actors to play the characters and allow the directors to experiment with the characters in action by trying different physical and vocal patterns. How is meaning altered if characters are located closer together or farther apart? Is the connotation different if words are spoken more slowly? What is suggested by a pause before a character speaks? Give directors the opportunity to compare different action patterns and decide which choices best express the story's meaning. As they try options, compare alternatives, evaluate them, and make choices, the directors are delving into the text in greater detail to enact the story with accuracy and meaning. Once again, remind readers that this is not a performance for an audience but a way to help them comprehend and see the story's action. They may find that some of their choices don't tell the story in the best way but lead them to stronger alternatives.

---

**Applicable Common Core Goals**

**CCSS.ELA-Literacy. CCSS.R.1**

Read closely to determine what the text says explicitly and to make logical inferences from it; cite specific textual evidence when writing or speaking to support conclusions drawn from the text.

**CCSS.ELA-Literacy. CCRA.R.2**

Determine central ideas or themes of a text and analyze their development; summarize the key supporting details and ideas.

**CCSS.ELA-Literacy. CCRA.R.4**

Interpret words and phrases as they are used in a text, including determining technical, connotative, and figurative meanings, and analyze how specific word choices shape meaning or tone.

---

**CCSS.ELA-Literacy. CCRA.R.5**

Analyze the structure of texts, including how specific sentences, paragraphs, and larger portions of the text (e.g., a section, chapter, scene, or stanza) relate to each other and the whole.

**CCSS.ELA-Literacy. CCRA.R.7**

Integrate and evaluate content presented in diverse media and formats, including visually and quantitatively, as well as in words.

**CCSS.ELA-Literacy. CCRA.SL.1**

Prepare for and participate effectively in a range of conversations and collaborations with diverse partners, building on others' ideas and expressing their own clearly and persuasively.

**CCSS.ELA-Literacy. CCRA.SL.2**

Integrate and evaluate information presented in diverse media and formats, including visually, quantitatively, and orally.

**CCSS.ELA-Literacy. CCRA.SL.4**

Present information, findings, and supporting evidence such that listeners can follow the line of reasoning and the organization, development, and style are appropriate to task, purpose, and audience.

The process of exploring the text as directors—searching for and recording the story's action, envisioning how it will be represented, and creating an enactment of it—transforms the reading process into one of inquiry, analysis, and synthesis. As students ask questions, try various options, compare them, evaluate them, and ultimately select the best way to represent the action of the literary work, they become both problem solvers and detectives, searching the text for specific details, building on it with their own imagination, and finding the best way to express its meaning physically and vocally.

# 4

# Reading Collaboratively

*Building Characters' Lives, Constructing Context, and Generating Action Together*

Reading the text collaboratively means dividing the artists' tasks among members of the class, having each group work independently, and then combining their work to achieve the ultimate goals. This is the model actually used in theatrical practice, as actors, designers, and directors all work together toward one unified stage production. Designers and directors consult and come to consensus so that the environment accommodates the story's action, directors and actors work together to ensure that the story's action reflects accurate character behaviors, and all of the artists collaborate to create a comprehensive production that presents the audience with a cohesive and interconnected story.

For me as a longtime practitioner of theater, this is my preferred method for applying these reading strategies in the classroom. I like for students to have responsibility both to the literature and to each other. This approach gives each group of students a specific set of individual reading tasks to accomplish as actors, designers, or directors, then integrates their work to complete the process of meaning making, thus engaging readers in a genuinely collaborative learning experience. Each group receives a worklist detailing specific tasks as actors, designers, or directors. After the groups complete their own tasks, they collaborate to integrate the story's characters, context, and action.

**Steps of Reading Collaboratively**

1. Divide the class into three groups and assign each group a worklist.

2. Designers and directors collaborate to envision the context and action.

3. Directors, designers, and actors collaborate to create the enactment in the context.

## Step 1: Divide the Class into Three Groups and Assign Each Group a Worklist

The first step of this process is to divide the class into three groups: actors, designers, and directors. You can divide the class randomly, select which students will make up each group of artists, or ask if students have a preference. I generally assign groups randomly to avoid any hint of favoritism.

The three groups—actors, designers, and directors—then each receive a worklist detailing the tasks for which they are responsible. These are the same worklists I use for each individual reading process, and you will see how students use them to work collaboratively in Section II, Application in the Classroom.

Each group begins by searching for and recording evidence from the text. The actors search the text for evidence of character, the designers for evidence of context, and the directors for evidence of action. The actors create character biographies and relationships and fill in any time gaps in the story line. The designers conceive and envision what the environment will look like in the classroom and consult with the directors to ensure that it will accommodate the story's action. The directors identify the sequence of actions in the story, and all three groups work together to construct the environment and enact the story's action in the classroom.

## Step 2: Designers and Directors Collaborate to Envision the Context and Action

Following initial work in their separate groups, the designers and directors meet to collaborate. The designers explain their idea for the environment, and the directors, who have envisioned the story's sequence of actions, determine whether the designers' environment will accommodate the action. The directors and designers solve any differences between them and come to a tentative consensus regarding an environment that will accommodate the story's action. They draw an accurate sketch of it.

## Step 3: Directors, Designers, and Actors Collaborate to Create the Enactment in the Context

The designers reconfigure the classroom and construct the environment on which they have agreed with the directors. The directors then collaborate with the actors to generate the action of the story. As the directors coach the actors through the sequence of actions and try different options, the designers make any adjustments needed in the environment to accommodate the action, and the actors work with the directors to ensure that the physical and verbal actions reflect the characters' objectives. In this way, the students all collaborate to achieve a unified whole. They ask each other questions, assess different options, and evaluate alternatives to determine how to combine character, context, and action to tell the story in the best way.

---

### Applicable Common Core Goals

**CCSS.ELA-Literacy. CCRA.R.1**

Read closely to determine what the text says explicitly and to make logical inferences from it; cite specific textual evidence when writing or speaking to support conclusions drawn from the text.

**CCSS.ELA-Literacy. CCRA.R.2**

Determine central ideas or themes of a text and analyze their development; summarize the key supporting details and ideas.

**CCSS.ELA-Literacy. CCRA.R.3**

Analyze how and why individuals, events, or ideas develop and interact over the course of a text.

**CCSS.ELA-Literacy. CCRA.R.4**

Interpret words and phrases as they are used in a text, including determining technical, connotative, and figurative meanings, and analyze how specific word choices shape meaning or tone.

**CCSS.ELA-Literacy. CCRA.R.5**

Analyze the structure of texts, including how specific sentences, paragraphs, and larger portions of the text (e.g., a section, chapter, scene, or stanza) relate to each other and the whole.

**CCSS.ELA-Literacy. CCRA.R.6**

Assess how point of view or purpose shapes the content and style of a text.

**CCSS.ELA-Literacy. CCRA.R.7**

Integrate and evaluate content presented in diverse media and formats, including visually and quantitatively, as well as in words.

**CCSS.ELA-Literacy. CCRA.R.8**

Delineate and evaluate the argument and specific claims in a text, including the validity of the reasoning as well as the relevance and sufficiency of the evidence.

**CCSS.ELA-Literacy. CCRA.W.1**

Write arguments to support claims in an analysis of substantive topics or texts using valid reasoning and relevant and sufficient evidence.

**CCSS.ELA-Literacy. CCRA.W.3**

Write narratives to develop real or imagined experiences or events using effective technique, well-chosen details, and well-structured event sequences.

**CCSS.ELA-Literacy. CCRA.SL.1**

Prepare for and participate effectively in a range of conversations and collaborations with diverse partners, building on others' ideas and expressing their own clearly and persuasively.

**CCSS.ELA-Literacy. CCRA.SL.2**

Integrate and evaluate information presented in diverse media and formats, including visually, quantitatively, and orally.

**CCSS.ELA-Literacy. CCRA.SL.3**

Evaluate a speaker's point of view, reasoning, and use of evidence and rhetoric.

**CCSS.ELA-Literacy. CCRA.SL.4**

Present information, findings, and supporting evidence such that listeners can follow the line of reasoning and the organization, development, and style are appropriate to task, purpose, and audience.

**CCSS.ELA-Literacy. CCRA.L.5**

Demonstrate understanding of figurative language, word relationships, and nuances in word meanings.

The collaborative reading process splits the focus on character, context, and action between the readers and asks them to combine resources to create the whole. One group of readers searches for and records *character* information, creates character biographies and relationships, and fills in any time gaps in the story line; another group searches for and records *context* information, envisions a context, and builds it into reality; and a third group searches for and records the story's *action*, envisions how it will be represented, and generates an enactment of it. Together, the groups find where the processes intersect and work collaboratively. Thus, while each group has specific tasks to accomplish, they all have a stake in the final outcome and must remain active participants throughout the entire process. Making readers responsible both to the text and to each other, the collaborative process challenges students to read responsibly, consult with each other, solve problems together, and work collectively in the process of making meaning.

# II

# Application in the Classroom

In this section, I will guide you through multiple applications of the theater artists' reading strategies as I have described them in Section I and as I have implemented them in middle school, high school, and community college classrooms. Using the short poem "Oranges" by Gary Soto and the short story "Thank You, M'am" by Langston Hughes[*] as mentor texts, I will describe various methods that I use to engage students in the actor's process, the designer's process, the director's process, and the collaborative process. Through accounts of classroom activity and examples of student work, you will see how these reading strategies facilitate more in-depth perception, meaning making, and comprehension and how each reading process focuses on certain aspects of the text, thus providing students with a variety of perspectives and multiple entry points into the literature.

Using these strategies, students read, answer questions, and complete tasks in the roles of theater artists. This technique—Dorothy Heathcote's mantle of the expert approach to teaching and learning—grants students the mantle or responsibility of the expert, in this case as theater artists, and creates a classroom environment in which students not only take in information but also apply it. In addition, I always work as the teacher-in-role by engaging with students as an executive actor, executive designer, executive director, or producer; focusing them on their reading tasks; and guiding them toward achieving their goals. As you place yourself "in role" with the students, you create the opportunity to model the behavior of a responsible actor, designer, or director and guide the students through the reading tasks. As you take your students through each process, model the steps by demonstrating how each is done, doing it with them, and letting them do it on their own. You will have to determine how much modeling and scaffolding your students need in order to accomplish the reading goals.

---

[*]You may find editions of this story titled "Thank You, M'am," "Thank You, Ma'am," or "Thank You Ma'm." We are using the text version licensed from Farrar, Straus and Giroux from *The Short Stories* by Langston Hughes, published by Farrar, Straus and Giroux /Hill and Wang. 1996.

For all of these classroom examples, I use a two-day time frame. However, some of them can be accomplished in one day, and others lend themselves to longer application if you have the time. Additionally, I always give students a worklist with questions to answer and tasks to accomplish to guide their reading. You will find the actor's worklist, the designer's worklist, and the director's worklist near the beginning of each appropriate chapter in this section. I use the same worklists for both of the mentor texts, and I use all three of the worklists for the collaborative process. Feel free to use these worklists for your students or adapt them to accommodate specific literature you are using. The worklists I use are also reprinted in the appendix.

There is no "right" way to apply these reading strategies in the classroom. Each strategy can be fully implemented or used partially, and readers can work either individually or in groups. These strategies are meant to be flexible and adaptable. Please apply them in your classroom in the way that best suits your time frame, the literature you are using, and your students.

## Front-Loading

There is a certain amount of front-loading you will need to do before you engage your students with these new reading strategies. Remember that you are teaching a language arts class and not a drama class, so you will need to orient your students before you begin any of these strategies. You don't need to do much, but it is important to prepare them for the fact that they will be engaging in something new and reading in a different way.

I usually begin with something like, "Today we are going to read a text, and then we are going to read it again in a totally different way." I always get strange looks when I say this, but I continue enthusiastically. I tell students we are going to borrow some reading ideas from the world of theater because people in the theater must read in a unique way to understand literature well enough to bring it to life on the stage. Actors in the theater read to build characters' lives, set designers read to imagine and construct context, and directors read to generate and implement the action of the text. I explain the difference between theater and drama and assure students that they are *not* going to turn the text into a stage production for an audience but will engage in a little role-playing and learn some new reading strategies that will give them a way to "see" and experience what they read. If you have students who have taken drama classes, ask them to help elaborate on the preparation process for a theatrical production. You will find that whatever they say, it will verify your assertion that reading for a theater artist is a *process*, a series of steps to achieve specific goals.

If I'm going to introduce only one of the reading strategies, I explain the reading process for that type of artist; if I'm going to apply all of the strategies and have the students work collaboratively, I describe each reading process and explain how they work together. You don't need to go into great detail about the theater in general or about actors, designers, and directors. Mainly, you want to orient the students to the fact that these artists read in distinctive ways in order to transform text into meaning for an audience. Look over the information in Section I, Reading as a Theater Artist, for information that will help you introduce your students to these new reading strategies. As you prepare your students for what they will be doing, let them know that as they learn these new reading strategies, they will not just be reading but *interacting with* the text, combining their own imaginative ideas with the writer's words to find meaning in the text.

I am including here the two mentor texts—"Oranges" by Gary Soto and "Thank You, M'am" by Langston Hughes—so that you can easily refer to them as you read accounts of classroom application of the reading strategies.

### Oranges

The first time I walked
With a girl, I was twelve,
Cold, and weighted down
With two oranges in my jacket.
December. Frost cracking
Beneath my steps, my breath
Before me, then gone,
As I walked toward
Her house, the one whose
Porch light burned yellow
Night and day, in any weather.
A dog barked at me, until
She came out pulling
At her gloves, face bright
With rouge. I smiled,
Touched her shoulder, and led
Her down the street, across
A used car lot and a line
Of newly planted trees,
Until we were breathing
Before a drugstore. We

Entered, the tiny bell
Bringing a saleslady
Down a narrow aisle of goods.
I turned to the candies
Tiered like bleachers,
And asked what she wanted -
Light in her eyes, a smile
Starting at the corners
Of her mouth. I fingered
A nickel in my pocket,
And when she lifted a chocolate
That cost a dime,
I didn't say anything.
I took the nickel from
My pocket, then an orange,
And set them quietly on
The counter. When I looked up,
The lady's eyes met mine,
And held them, knowing
Very well what it was all
About.

    Outside,
A few cars hissing past,
Fog hanging like old
Coats between the trees.
I took my girl's hand
in mine for two blocks,
Then released it to let
Her unwrap the chocolate.
I peeled my orange
That was so bright against
The gray of December
That, from some distance,
Someone might have thought
I was making a fire in my hands.
—*Gary Soto*

**Thank You, M'am**

She was a large woman with a large purse that had everything in it but a hammer and nails. It had a long strap, and she carried it slung across her shoulder. It was about eleven o'clock at night, dark, and she was walking alone, when a boy ran up behind her and tried to snatch her purse. The strap broke with the sudden single tug the boy gave it from behind. But the boy's weight and the weight of the purse combined caused him to lose his balance. Instead of taking off full blast as he had hoped, the boy fell on his back on the sidewalk and his legs flew up. The large woman simply turned around and kicked him right square in his blue-jeaned sitter. Then she reached down, picked the boy up by his shirtfront, and shook him until his teeth rattled.

After that the woman said, "Pick up my pocketbook, boy, and give it here."

She still held him tightly. But she bent down enough to permit him to stoop and pick up her purse. Then she said, "Now ain't you ashamed of yourself?"

Firmly gripped by his shirtfront, the boy said, "Yes'm."

The woman said, "What did you want to do it for?"

The boy said, "I didn't aim to."

She said, "You a lie!"

By that time two or three people passed, stopped, turned to look, and some stood watching.

"If I turn you loose, will you run?" asked the woman.

"Yes'm," said the boy.

"Then I won't turn you loose," said the woman. She did not release him.

"Lady, I'm sorry," whispered the boy.

"Um-hum! Your face is dirty. I got a great mind to wash your face for you. Ain't you got nobody home to tell you to wash your face?"

"No'm," said the boy.

"Then it will get washed this evening," said the large woman, starting up the street, dragging the frightened boy behind her.

He looked as if he were fourteen or fifteen, frail and willow-wild, in tennis shoes and blue jeans.

The woman said, "You ought to be my son. I would teach you right from wrong. Least I can do right now is to wash your face. Are you hungry?"

"No'm," said the being-dragged boy. "I just want you to turn me loose."

"Was I bothering *you* when I turned that corner?" asked the woman.

"No'm."

"But you put yourself in contact with *me*," said the woman. "If you think that that contact is not going to last awhile, you got another thought coming. When I get through with you, sir, you are going to remember Mrs. Luella Bates Washington Jones."

Sweat popped out on the boy's face and he began to struggle. Mrs. Jones stopped, jerked him around in front of her, put a half nelson about his neck, and continued to drag him up the street. When she got to her door, she dragged the boy inside, down a hall, and into a large kitchenette-furnished room at the rear of the house. She switched on the light and left the door open. The boy could hear other roomers laughing and talking in the large house. Some of their doors were open, too, so he knew he and the woman were not alone. The woman still had him by the neck in the middle of her room.

She said, "What is your name?"

"Roger," answered the boy.

"Then, Roger, you go to that sink and wash your face," said the woman, whereupon she turned him loose—at last. Roger looked at the door—looked at the woman—looked at the door—*and went to the sink.*

"Let the water run until it gets warm," she said. "Here's a clean towel."

"You gonna take me to jail?" asked the boy, bending over the sink.

"Not with that face, I would not take you nowhere," said the woman. "Here I am trying to get home to cook me a bite to eat, and you snatch my pocketbook! Maybe you ain't been to your supper either, late as it be. Have you?"

"There's nobody home at my house," said the boy.

"Then we'll eat," said the woman. "I believe you're hungry—or been hungry—to try to snatch my pocketbook!"

"I want a pair of blue suede shoes," said the boy.

"Well, you didn't have to snatch *my* pocketbook to get some suede shoes," said Mrs. Luella Bates Washington Jones. "You could've asked me."

"M'am?"

The water dripping from his face, the boy looked at her. There was a long pause. A very long pause. After he had dried his face and not knowing what else to do, dried it again, the boy turned around, wondering what next. The door was open. He could make a dash for it down the hall. He could run, run, run, *run!*

The woman was sitting on the daybed. After a while she said, "I were young once and I wanted things I could not get."

There was another long pause. The boy's mouth opened. Then he frowned, not knowing he frowned.

The woman said, "Um-hum! You thought I was going to say *but,* didn't you? You thought I was going to say, *but I didn't snatch people's pocketbooks.* Well, I wasn't going to say that." Pause. Silence. "I have done things, too, which I would not tell you, son—neither tell God, if He didn't already know. Everybody's got something in common. So you set down while I fix us something to eat. You might run that comb through your hair so you will look presentable."

In another corner of the room behind a screen was a gas plate and an icebox. Mrs. Jones got up and went behind the screen. The woman did not watch the boy to see if he was going to run now, nor did she watch her purse, which she left behind her on the daybed. But the boy took care to sit on the far side of the room, away from the purse, where he thought she could easily see him out of the corner of her eye if she wanted to. He did not trust the woman *not* to trust him. And he did not want to be mistrusted now.

"Do you need somebody to go to the store," asked the boy, "maybe to get some milk or something?"

"Don't believe I do," said the woman, "unless you just want sweet milk yourself. I was going to make cocoa out of this canned milk I got here."

"That will be fine," said the boy.

She heated some lima beans and ham she had in the icebox, made the cocoa, and set the table. The woman did not ask the boy anything about where he lived, or his folks, or anything else that would embarrass him. Instead, as they ate, she told him about her job in a hotel beauty shop that stayed open late, what the work was like, and how all kinds of women came in and out, blondes, redheads, and Spanish. Then she cut him a half of her ten-cent cake.

"Eat some more, son," she said.

When they were finished eating, she got up and said, "Now here, take this ten dollars and buy yourself some blue suede shoes. And next time, do not make the mistake of latching onto *my* pocketbook *nor nobody else's*—because shoes got by devilish ways will burn your feet. I got to get my rest now. But from here on in, son, I hope you will behave yourself."

She led him down the hall to the front door and opened it. "Good night! Behave yourself, boy!" she said, looking out into the street as he went down the steps.

The boy wanted to say something other than, "Thank you, m'am," to Mrs. Luella Bates Washington Jones, but although his lips moved, he couldn't even say that as he turned at the foot of the barren stoop and looked up at the large woman in the door. Then she shut the door.

—Langston Hughes

# 5

# Application of the Actor's Process

## *Building Characters' Lives*

T he actor's process is probably the easiest to apply on its own. Students can work individually or in groups to find character evidence within a text, create character biographies and relationships, and fill in any time gaps in the story line. The approach I describe here with the mentor texts is a two-day process. You can condense it into one day if you have readers search the text and accomplish the writing tasks as quick-writes, or you can extend it with longer and more involved writing assignments. The length of time you take and how you apply this process will depend on the ability of your students, the complexity of the literature with which you are working, and your own preferences.

## Students Build Characters' Lives with "Oranges"

### *Day One*

I always start with front-loading and inform the students that they will be doing something different with reading in the next two days. I explain that we will be borrowing some ideas from the world of theater, where artists must understand the text in great detail in order to transform it into a stage production. More specifically, I describe how we will focus on the reading strategies that *actors* use to help them delve deeper into a text and create the lives of characters. I assure students that they will not be acting for an audience but will be using the actor's reading strategies to find character details in the text and apply their own imagination to build the specifics of the characters' lives.

After this orientation, I give each student a copy of "Oranges" and provide some background on the poem and the writer, Gary Soto. We read the poem aloud together "as ourselves." Then I ask if they would be willing to read the poem again but this time engage in a little role-playing with me and read it as actors. I also tell them that I will assume the role of executive actor to guide them toward their reading goals as actors. They all think being actors is very glamorous and agree to give it a try.

I tell students that as we read as actors, we will have three specific reading goals:

1. Search for and record evidence of character from the text.

2. Generate character biographies and relationships.

3. Fill in any time gaps in the story line.

Next, I hand out and review the actor's worklist, which specifies exactly what students need to accomplish, to make sure they know what their goals are as they read.

---

**The Actor's Worklist**

**A.** Search for and record evidence of character from the text.

   1. What is the full name of each character in the text?

   2. What does the text explicitly tell you about each character?

   3. What is the age, date of birth, and place of birth of each character?

   4. Where do the characters live?

   5. What are the important traits of each character?

   6. What are the relationships between the characters at the beginning of the text?

   7. What are the relationships between the characters at the end of the text?

   8. What happens to make the characters different by the end of the text?

   9. Are there any time gaps in the story line?

**B.** Combine the character evidence you have found in the text with your own imagination to write a biography of each character.

**C.** Combine the character evidence you have found in the text with your own imagination to write about the characters' relationships.

**D.** Combine the character evidence you have found in the text with your own imagination to fill in any time gaps in the story line.

---

We now begin our reading as actors.

## Step 1: Search for and Record Evidence of Character from the Text

With the worklist, students have very specific questions to answer as they search for character evidence. I try to craft the questions on the worklist in a way that will guide students toward ultimately writing character biographies, establishing relationships between the characters, and filling in any time gaps in the story line. I tell them they will find some of the answers they need explicitly embedded in the text but other questions will ask them to determine information that the writer has not specified. This prompt starts them on the process of hypothesizing from evidence in the text. I explain that any speculation they make about the characters' lives must be based on evidence from the text. I use the opportunity to discuss the fact that different readers make different choices, which is fine as long as their conclusions are logical and based on textual evidence.

Students can accomplish their search for evidence individually or in small groups. You can have everyone in the class search for character evidence for all of the characters, or you can divide the characters among the students. For this unit on "Oranges," I divide them into three groups and ask each group to search for character evidence for one of the three characters.

I give students the option of a variety of note-taking methods. Some record information they find directly onto the written text; some take notes on a tablet, laptop, or blank sheet of paper; and others use a worksheet (see Figures 5.1 and 5.2). The actor's worksheets I use to help students record evidence from the text are included in the appendix; of course, you can also create your own. Since "Oranges" is short, I give them ten minutes to complete their search for character evidence, then ask each group to share what they have discovered about their character.

### WHAT THEY FIND

Students find character evidence embedded in the text of "Oranges" but also realize that they need to make inferences based on the text to answer many of the questions. Following their search for evidence, I lead them in a focused discussion about the three characters.

1.  *What is the full name of each character in the text?*

    Students find three characters in the poem, the narrator, the girl, and the saleslady, but discover that they are not given specific names. We discuss how this might contribute to the universality of the story.

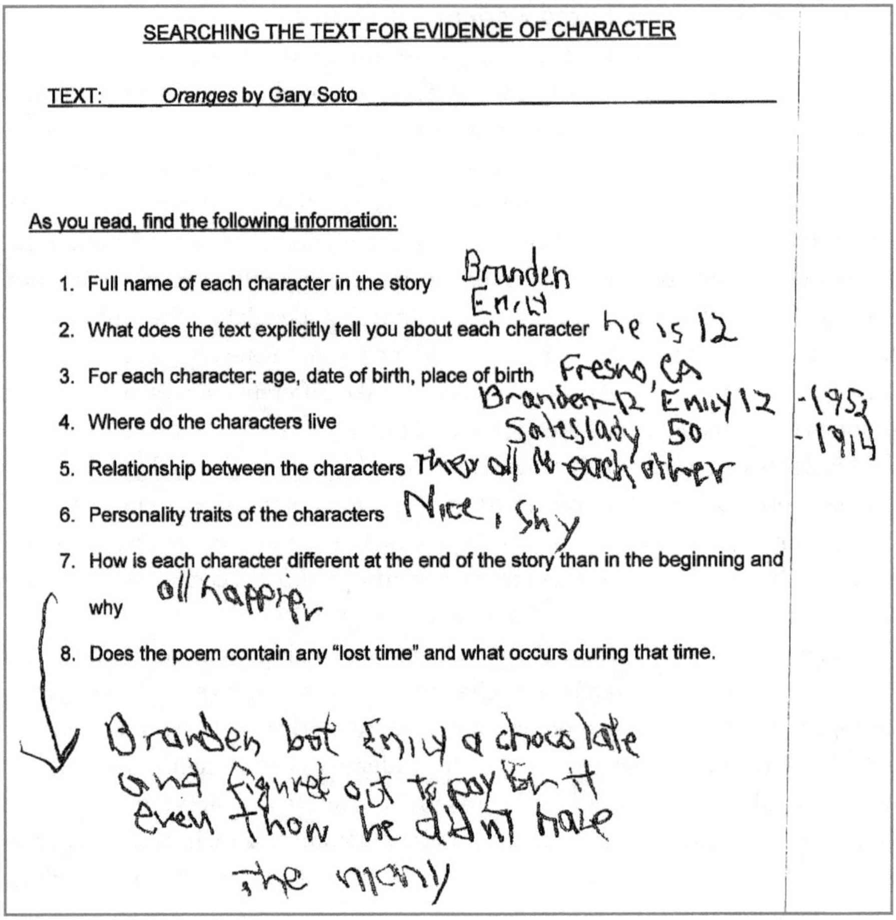

SEARCHING THE TEXT FOR EVIDENCE OF CHARACTER

TEXT: *Oranges* by Gary Soto

As you read, find the following information:

1. Full name of each character in the story Branden Emily
2. What does the text explicitly tell you about each character he is 12
3. For each character: age, date of birth, place of birth Fresno, CA Branden 12 Emily 12 -1952 Saleslady 50 -1914
4. Where do the characters live
5. Relationship between the characters They all [illegible] each other
6. Personality traits of the characters Nice, Shy
7. How is each character different at the end of the story than in the beginning and why all happier
8. Does the poem contain any "lost time" and what occurs during that time.

Branden bot Emily a chocolate and figured out to pay for it even thow he didnt have the many

**FIGURE 5.1.** Using a worksheet to record character evidence.

2. *What does the text explicitly tell you about each character?*

The narrator is twelve years old ("The first time I walked / With a girl, I was twelve").

The girl wears rouge ("face bright / With rouge").

The saleslady works in a drugstore ("Bringing a saleslady / Down a narrow aisle of goods").

3. *What is the age, date of birth, and place of birth of each character?*

Since the text does not provide that information, this is where students begin to make inferences. The text states that the narrator is twelve years

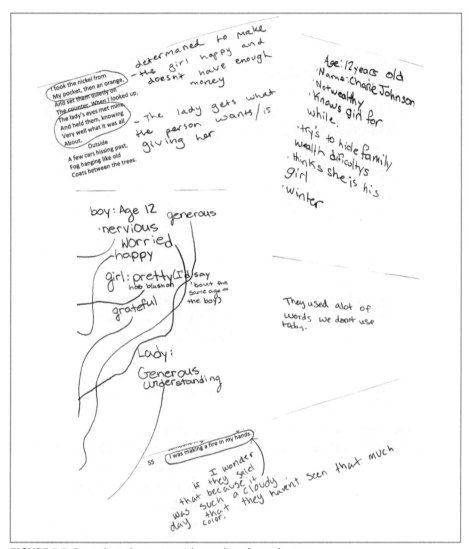

The following annotations appear on the figure:

determaned to make the girl happy and doesn't have enough money

I took the nickel from My pocket, then an orange, And set them quietly on The counter. When I looked up, The lady's eyes met mine, And held them, knowing Very well what it was all About. Outside A few cars hissing past, Fog hanging like old Coats between the trees.

- The lady gets what the person wants / is giving her

Age: 12 years old
Name: Chane Johnson
Not wealthy
Knows girl for while.
try's to hide family wealth dificoltys
thinks she is his girl
winter

boy: Age 12 generous
nervious
Worried
happy

girl: pretty (I'd say has blush on 'bout the same age as the boy)
grateful

They used alot of words we don't use today.

Lady:
Generous
understanding

55 I was making a fire in my hands.

I wonder if they said that because it was such a cloudy day that color. they haven't seen that much

**FIGURE 5.2.** Recording character evidence directly on the text.

old. I prompt students with the fact that writer Gary Soto was born in 1952 and is from central California. They speculate that the writer might be projecting himself into the story as the narrator and reason that if he were born in 1952, then the action of the poem would take place in 1964. No location for the narrator's birth is specified, but students note that the action takes place somewhere with "Frost cracking / Beneath my steps, my breath / Before me, then gone" and "Fog hanging like old / Coats between the trees." This setting could possibly be located in central California. Students speculate that the narrator has probably lived in this place his whole life.

The girl's age is not stated. Students think she is most likely the same age as the narrator and from the same place.

The saleslady's age is also unstated, but students think she seems older and wiser ("The lady's eyes met mine, / And held them, knowing / Very well what it was all / About"). Students think she might be around fifty, therefore born in 1914, probably in the same place. Some students think she is older and some younger, which leads to an interesting discussion about choices based on textual evidence. As students justify answers, they continually refer back to the text to find evidence to verify their choices.

4. *Where do the characters live?*

Generally, students think all three of the characters were born in the same place and have lived there their whole lives. They think it is probably in central California, since that is where the writer is from. We explore why they think that and what textual evidence supports it. We also locate central California on a map.

5. *What are the important traits of each character?*

Students think the narrator is a little forward with the girl ("Touched her shoulder" and "took my girl's hand / in mine for two blocks") given that this is the first time he has taken her out ("The first time I walked / With a girl"). They also think the narrator does not have much money since he has only a nickel in the pocket of the jacket. They note that the narrator is a quick thinker ("I took the nickel from / My pocket, then an orange, / And set them quietly on / The counter"). One student questions the gender of the narrator and asks if it has to be a boy. We reread the poem and discover that there is no reference to the narrator's gender; as a result, I refer to the narrator in ungendered terms from here on.

Students think the girl has lived in this place her whole life and views going out with the narrator as special, given the rouge on her cheeks.

They think the saleslady has also lived in this place her whole life and has worked at the drugstore since she was eighteen years old. Some think the drugstore is owned by her family. They also think she has no children of her own, which is why she loves the neighborhood children so much.

6. *What are the relationships between the characters at the beginning of the text?*

   Students think the narrator and the girl know each other since the narrator comes to her house to pick her up. They also think that the two are probably friends at school and that the saleslady is not related to either of them but knows them from the neighborhood. Some think the saleslady is the narrator's aunt, since she is so nice to the narrator and accepts the orange as part of the payment for the chocolate. This speculation leads to a preliminary discussion about why the saleslady accepted the narrator's payment.

7. *What are the relationships between the characters at the end of the text?*

   Students think the narrator is more confident because the encounter with the girl ultimately went well. They generally decide that the girl really likes the narrator, though some think she finds the narrator boring. In discussion, students cannot find explicit evidence to support either view, and they realize that because the poem is written from the point of view of the narrator, we don't know much about what the girl is thinking. Discussion ensues about point of view and how the poem might be different if written from the girl's perspective. Students agree that the saleslady is pleased that she performed a good deed.

8. *What happens to make the characters different by the end of the text?*

   Students decide that the narrator found a way to solve a major problem and is very pleased and happy that the girl never knew about the potential trouble. Most think the girl likes the narrator and is thrilled that the narrator bought the chocolate for her, and they agree that the saleslady is happy she accepted the narrator's payment and prevented embarrassment.

9. *Are there any time gaps in the story line?*

   Students speculate that when the narrator and the girl exit the drugstore ("Outside"), the narrator, if he is a boy, opens the door for the girl. They think so because it was the custom in the era they have determined for the poem's setting.

In this way, our search for evidence, guided and focused by the questions, yields basic information that we can now build on to generate character biographies and character relationships.

### Step 2: Generate Character Biographies and Relationships

Now, students must delve deeper into the text, use their imagination, and become even more active in the reading process. They must build on evidence they have found in the text and fill in details of characters' lives as they create character biographies and explore character relationships (see Figure 5.3).

For this step, I keep students in the same groups and ask each student to write a one-page biography of the character with which they have been working. Additionally, I assign the members of one group to write one page about the relationship between the narrator and the girl, another group to write about the relationship between the narrator and the saleslady, and the third group to write about the relationship between the saleslady and the girl. Students use the rest of the class period to get started on their writing, which they will complete as homework.

## Day Two

### Step 2: Generate Character Biographies and Relationships

As the students come into the classroom on day two, they get back into their groups to share the biographies and character relationships they have written. I remind them that there is no single "correct" biography for any character or "right" description of character relationships. I start the class by giving students fifteen minutes to share their biographies, compare what they have written, and select one biography to read to the class. I visit each group to hear some of their writing and help them stay on task. I then give them another ten minutes to share their character relationship writings with each other and again select one to read to class. Meanwhile, I visit each group again. Each group then shares their two selections with the class.

### Step 3: Fill in Any Time Gaps in the Story Line

Since "Oranges" has only one very short time gap, I ask the class to identify that gap and postulate about what occurs during it. Students quickly identify it—the short time between when the narrator pays for the chocolate and when the nar-

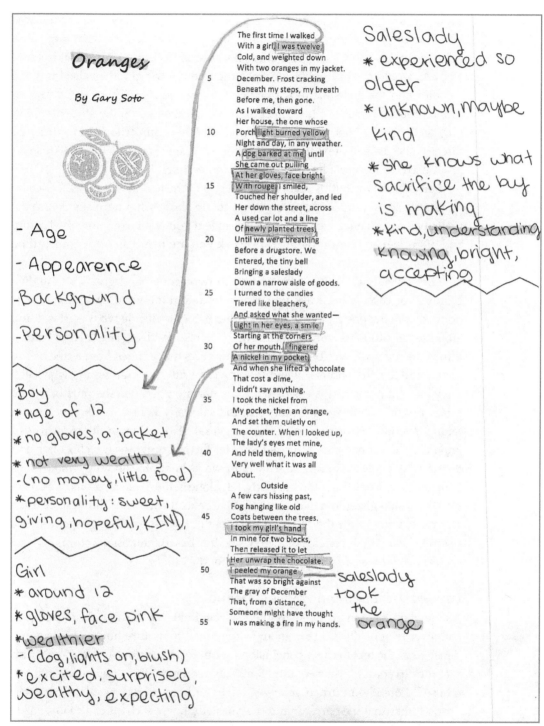

**Oranges**

By Gary Soto

- Age
- Appearence
- Background
- Personality

Boy
*age of 12
*no gloves, a jacket
*not very wealthy
-(no money, little food)
*personality: sweet,
giving, hopeful, KIND,

Girl
*around 12
*gloves, face pink
*wealthier
-(dog, lights on, blush)
*excited, surprised,
wealthy, expecting

The first time I walked
With a girl, I was twelve,
Cold, and weighted down
With two oranges in my jacket.
5  December. Frost cracking
Beneath my steps, my breath
Before me, then gone.
As I walked toward
Her house, the one whose
10  Porch light burned yellow
Night and day, in any weather.
A dog barked at me, until
She came out pulling
At her gloves, face bright
15  With rouge, I smiled,
Touched her shoulder, and led
Her down the street, across
A used car lot and a line
Of newly planted trees,
20  Until we were breathing
Before a drugstore. We
Entered, the tiny bell
Bringing a saleslady
Down a narrow aisle of goods.
25  I turned to the candies
Tiered like bleachers,
And asked what she wanted—
Light in her eyes, a smile
Starting at the corners
30  Of her mouth. I fingered
A nickel in my pocket,
And when she lifted a chocolate
That cost a dime,
I didn't say anything.
35  I took the nickel from
My pocket, then an orange,
And set them quietly on
The counter. When I looked up,
The lady's eyes met mine,
40  And held them, knowing
Very well what it was all
About.
            Outside
A few cars hissing past,
Fog hanging like old
45  Coats between the trees.
I took my girl's hand
In mine for two blocks,
Then released it to let
Her unwrap the chocolate.
50  I peeled my orange
That was so bright against
The gray of December
That, from a distance,
Someone might have thought
55  I was making a fire in my hands.

Saleslady
* experienced so
older
* unknown, maybe
kind
* she knows what
sacrifice the boy
is making
* kind, understanding,
knowing, bright,
accepting

saleslady
took
the
orange

**FIGURE 5.3.** Evidence gathered from the text toward writing character biographies.

rator and the girl are outside the drugstore ("knowing / Very well what it was all / About. // Outside, / A few cars hissing past"). I ask them what they think happens in this short gap. Most think, because of the era, that if the narrator is a boy he would be very polite and open the door for the girl; they also think the narrator and the girl start to walk once they get outside. There are, however, different ideas regarding the direction in which they go. Some students think they walk directly back to the girl's house, but others think they go in a different direction because the text this time mentions "A few cars hissing past" instead of "A used car lot and a line / Of newly planted trees."

Since there is only this one short time gap in the text of "Oranges," I decide to allocate some time for students to speculate about what happens before the poem begins and after it ends. You can decide if you want to explore the "before and after" depending on the literary work you are using and how much time you have.

For this activity, I divide the class into two groups and give students five minutes for discussion. I ask one group to determine what each character is doing before the poem begins and the other group to decide what each is doing after it ends. Students come up with some interesting ideas. The "before" group thinks the narrator lives on an orchard and picks the oranges from a tree before walking to the girl's house "weighted down / With two oranges in my jacket." They also think the girl is eager to see the narrator, because she puts on rouge ("face bright / With rouge") and that the saleslady is busy in the back room taking inventory ("the tiny bell / Bringing a saleslady / Down a narrow aisle of goods"). The "after" group thinks that after the girl unwraps her chocolate and the narrator peels the orange, the narrator walks her home and they make plans to meet again. They think the saleslady, left alone in the drugstore, places a nickel into the cash register to make up for the five cents the narrator didn't have, then eats the orange. While the "after" group does not cite specific language from the poem to justify their conclusions, they say they based their assumptions on how each character was affected by the actions of the others.

## DELVING DEEPER: FINDING MORE MEANING

As members of each group share their selected biographies and descriptions of character relationships, I stop them as they read to inquire how they used evidence from the text to draw conclusions about the characters. One group claims that the girl comes from a wealthy family, based on the line "Her house, the one whose / Porchlight burned yellow / Night and day, in any weather." Another group thinks that the narrator and the saleslady knew each other already, based on the line "The lady's eyes met mine / And held them, knowing / Very well what it was all / About." If we hear claims that are not supported by textual evidence, we collectively look back into the text to justify assertions or conclude that a particular claim is not valid as part of a character's biography or relationship to another character.

## Students Build Characters' Lives with "Thank You, M'am"

### Day One

I begin the actor's process for Langston Hughes's short story "Thank You, M'am" in the same way as for "Oranges," by informing the students that we will be doing something very different with reading today and tomorrow. Each student receives a copy of the story, we read it aloud together "as ourselves," and I give students some background on the story and the author. I now tell students that we will read the story again but this time use a little role-playing and read it as actors. I explain that I will participate in the process with them as executive actor.

Thinking they will all become stars, they agree.

I tell them that we are going to borrow some reading strategies from the world of the theater. I describe how theater artists must read text in a special way to transform literary works into stage productions, and I tell them we are

going to concentrate on the reading strategies that *actors* use to build characters' lives. They will have three reading goals:

1. Search for and record evidence of character from the text.
2. Generate character biographies and relationships.
3. Fill in any time gaps in the story line.

I give them the actor's worklist (the same as for "Oranges") specifying the tasks they need to accomplish and the goals they need to work toward as they read. I ask if they are ready to read the story again, no longer as students and teacher in a classroom, but as actors. I remind them that I am working with them in role as the executive actor whose job is to help them reach their reading goals. We begin our reading process as actors.

## Step 1: Search for and Record Evidence of Character from the Text

Instead of asking students to work in groups, I ask them to search individually for evidence related to both characters. I give them twenty minutes to complete this part of the actor's process, reminding them to take notes about what they discover. Some write notes directly on the text, others take notes on a screen or blank sheet of paper, and some use a worksheet (for an example, see Figure 5.4).

### WHAT THEY FIND

As students conduct their search for evidence, they discover a great deal of information explicitly stated in the text but also find that they must infer from the text to answer many of the questions. Following their search for evidence, I lead students in a discussion of the two characters, during which they share what they have discovered in the text and explain how they used evidence from the text to make inferences.

1. *What is the full name of each character in the text?*

   Students find that "Thank You, M'am" has two main characters: Mrs. Luella Bates Washington Jones and Roger. The writer does not specify Roger's last name, and individual students choose different last names for him. They also find several incidental characters, including those who watch the action in the street ("By that time two or three people passed, stopped, turned to look, and some stood watching") and some additional roomers at the boardinghouse ("The boy could hear other roomers laughing and talking in the large house"). They decide these characters don't need names.

# *Thank You, Ma'am (by Langston Hughes)*

She was a large woman with a large purse that had everything in it but hammer and nails. It had a long strap, and she carried it slung across her shoulder. It was about eleven o'clock at night, and she was walking alone, when a boy ran up behind her and tried to snatch her purse. The strap broke with the single tug the boy gave it from behind. But the boy's weight and the weight of the purse combined caused him to lose his balance so, intsead of taking off full blast as he had hoped, the boy fell on his back on the sidewalk, and his legs flew up. the large woman simply turned around and kicked him right square in his blue-jeaned sitter. Then she reached down, picked the boy up by his shirt front, and shook him until his teeth rattled.

After that the woman said, "Pick up my pocketbook, boy, and give it here." She still held him. But she bent down enough to permit him to stoop and pick up her purse. Then she said, "Now ain't you ashamed of yourself?"

Firmly gripped by his shirt front, the boy said, "Yes'm."          *She is Strong*

The woman said, "What did you want to do it for?"

The boy said, "I didn't aim to."          *he is scared*

She said, "You a lie!"

By that time two or three people passed, stopped, turned to look, and some stood watching.

"If I turn you loose, will you run?" asked the woman.

"Yes'm," said the boy.

"Then I won't turn you loose," said the woman. She did not release him.

"I'm very sorry, lady, I'm sorry," whispered the boy.

"Um-hum! And your face is dirty. I got a great mind to wash your face for you. Ain't you got          *Boys face is dirty*
nobody home to tell you to wash your face?"

"No'm," said the boy.

"Then it will get washed this evening," said the large woman starting up the street, dragging the frightened boy behind her.

He looked as if he were fourteen or fifteen, frail and willow-wild, in tennis shoes and blue jeans.          *Boys age*

The woman said, "You ought to be my son. I would teach you right from wrong. Least I can do right now is to wash your face. Are you hungry?"

"No'm," said the being dragged boy. "I just want you to turn me loose."

"Was I bothering *you* when I turned that corner?" asked the woman.

"No'm."

**FIGURE 5.4.** Notes about character taken directly on the text.

2. *What does the text explicitly tell you about each character?*

Students find considerable information embedded directly in the text. They discover that Mrs. Jones is a "large woman" who states her full name: "When I get through with you, sir, you are going to remember Mrs. Luella Bates Washington Jones." They also discover that Roger is identified only by his first name: "She said, 'What is your name?' 'Roger,' answered the boy." The text tells them that Mrs. Jones works late hours at a beauty shop in a hotel: "she told him about her job in a hotel beauty shop that stayed open late, what the work was like, and how all kinds of women came in and out." The text also says that Roger's face is dirty and estimates his age: "fourteen or fifteen, frail and willow-wild, in tennis shoes and blue jeans." The text reveals where Mrs. Jones lives: "a large kitchenette-furnished room at the rear of the house." It does not state where Roger lives, although students do discover that he has no one at home to take care of him: "'Ain't you got nobody home to tell you to wash your face?' 'No'm.'"

3. *What is the age, date of birth, and place of birth of each character?*

Here, students begin to speculate and infer from the text. They find Roger's age in the text ("fourteen or fifteen") but no stated age for Mrs. Jones. Most readers think she is an older lady, in her sixties or seventies, and we discuss why they think so. I have told students that the short story was first published in 1958, and we speculate that it is set in that time. They figure that Roger was born in 1942 or 1943, and if Mrs. Jones is 65, then she was born in 1893. They note that the writer does not identify where either character was born, but, knowing that Langston Hughes grew up in the Midwest, they speculate that the characters are from somewhere in that region.

4. *Where do the characters live?*

Students find that the writer does not identify a specific location for the action. Some think that both characters probably still live in the town where they were born; others are unsure, which leads to discussion. Since we find no specific textual evidence of the location, we decide that the location may not be crucial, and the story could happen anywhere in the US.

5. *What are the important traits of each character?*

Students discover that qualities of each character are reflected in their behavior. When Roger attempts to steal her purse, Mrs. Jones stops him and takes him home to feed him instead of turning him over to the police. This action reveals her kindness and willingness to help rather than punish the young boy. Students wonder where she learned to use a half nelson, and they speculate about something in her youth that might have affected her actions in the story: "I were young once and I wanted things I could not get." Roger, though he tries to steal the woman's purse and is unwillingly dragged to her house, displays the behavior of a respectable boy rather than a renegade, as he opts to stay rather than run away when he has the chance. He even offers to go to the store for her: "Do you need somebody to go to the store . . . maybe to get some milk or something?"

6. *What are the relationships between the characters at the beginning of the text?*

Students find no evidence that the two main characters know each other before the action of the story begins. They first meet when Mrs. Jones is walking home late at night and Roger tries to steal her purse.

7. *What are the relationships between the characters at the end of the text?*

By the end of the story, the characters form a bond. Roger develops a respect for Mrs. Jones because of the kindness she has shown to him. Mrs. Jones hopes that she has taught Roger an important lesson about life and responsible behavior.

8. *What happens to make the characters different by the end of the text?*

This question leads students to discuss how the actions of each character affect the other character. Mrs. Jones takes Roger home and feeds him instead of taking him to the police station, and Roger doesn't run away from her when he has the chance. Students speculate that Mrs. Jones is satisfied with her actions and hopes she has made a difference in Roger's life. They think Roger is very affected by Mrs. Jones's kindness, since he may never have experienced that kind of behavior toward him and isn't quite sure what it means.

During this discussion, I continually prompt students to point to the textual evidence on which they base their speculations.

9.  *Are there any time gaps in the story line?*

*No.* The story moves from the beginning to the end without any time gaps.

## Step 2: Generate Character Biographies and Relationships

Students are now ready to *apply* the evidence they have found to write biographies of the characters and develop their relationships. I divide the class into three groups and instruct the students to write individually. One group is assigned to write biographies of Mrs. Jones, another group to write biographies of Roger, and the third group to write about the relationship between the two characters. This approach will give us the opportunity to compare ideas tomorrow. Students begin this assigned writing in class and will finish it as homework.

## *Day Two*

## Step 2: Generate Character Biographies and Relationships

As we begin day two, we continue our work with character biographies and relationships. Students meet in their three groups again and share their individual writing with each other (for examples, see Figures 5.5, 5.6, and 5.7). I visit each group and hear a great deal of variety in how they have constructed character biographies and relationships from textual evidence and what they have inferred from it.

### DELVING DEEPER: FINDING MORE MEANING

As I work with each group, I ask students to justify the conclusions they have drawn with textual evidence. In a discussion of the characters' relationship, one student hypothesizes that Roger reminds Mrs. Jones of a younger version of herself: "I have done things, too, which I would not tell you, son—neither tell God, if He didn't already know." The student thinks that Mrs. Jones was once caught shoplifting, was sent to jail, and now wants to teach Roger a lesson about kindness instead of punishment. Perhaps she wishes someone had done that for her. Several biographies of Roger theorize that despite his bad behavior of purse snatching, he really has a good heart: "Do you need somebody to go to the store . . . maybe to get some milk or something?"

Each group then selects one written piece to share with the class, and as we listen I prompt students to cite the evidence from the text on which they have based their conclusions. The biographies give us much more detail about each character, and the writings about their relationship help us understand how the characters affect each other.

**WORKSHEET 5:**

Literary Work ___Thank___

Actors: ___Piper___, Olivia, **Rya**, Becca, Ronin, Holly, Haley, Chase

Character Biography: **Roger** — Chase

| Date and Place of Birth/Age in Story | Chicago, 14 |
|---|---|
| Parents | Sarafina George } Johnson |
| Siblings | |
| Childhood Memories | The Streets / Stealing |
| Education | Street Smarts |
| Work History | Stealing |
| Important Relationships | None in the Beginning |
| Significant Life events | Meeting Mrs. Jones Kind |

**FIGURE 5.5.** Character biography worksheet.

Written Character Biography of Roger:

Roger Johnson born in inner city (Chicago) was never fully given the love his young self needed. His parents made ends meat barely scraping by. They never had enough to buy him anything so he learned at a young age what he doesn't have he takes. He spends most of his time in the street unable to bear his parents fighting. He's had his eyes on blue suede shoes for years. Knowing he cannot ask his parents Roger goes on a theft, quest for $10 dollars. He needs to steal his way to the shoes. There is only one problem, He still is terrible at stealing wallets and purses.

**FIGURE 5.6.** Written character biography.

---

**WORKSHEET 6:**

Literary Work "Thank You, Ma'am"

Actors: Haley, Becca, Aya, Piper, Olivia, Nicky, Haley, Holly, Ronin

| Characters | Present Relationship | Past Relationship | Relationship change in the story |
|---|---|---|---|
| • Mrs. Luella Bates Washington Jones<br><br>• Roger Johnson<br><br>• Street bystanders<br><br>• Fellow housemates | • Mrs. Jones has maternal feelings towards Roger<br><br>• Mrs. Jones sees herself in the young Roger<br><br>• Roger is grateful for her kindess | • They did not know each other, but they share a similar past<br><br>• Originally, she was upset because he tried to steal her pocket book | • She is mad at his disrespect and lack of compassion<br><br>• She realizes that they had a similar childhood and relates to him<br><br>• She is kind and feeds and helps clean him |

**FIGURE 5.7.** Character relationships worksheet.

## Step 3: Fill in Any Time Gaps in the Story Line

We determine that "Thank You, M'am" has no internal time gaps, so, for this step, I opt to have the students speculate about what occurs before and after the action of the story. Giving them five minutes to accomplish this task, I divide them into six small groups and ask three groups to discuss what happens before the story begins and three groups to discuss what happens after the story ends. As with "Oranges," this approach gives us the opportunity to compare a variety of ideas.

One group thinks the meeting between the two characters is random, and another thinks Roger has planned it. Some think Mrs. Jones says goodbye to her last client at the hair salon ("she told him about her job in a hotel beauty shop that stayed open late"), locks the door, starts walking home, and passes Roger, who is looking through the window of a shoe store. When he sees her walk by, Roger decides that she would be a good purse-snatching victim since she is an old lady and has such a large purse, and then he follows her. Some students think that Roger has been watching her walk the same route every night and is waiting for the best opportunity to snatch her purse.

After much discussion about the end of the story, in which Roger goes down the steps and Mrs. Jones closes the door, some readers conclude that Roger goes back to the shoe store, finds it closed, and goes to sleep on a park bench. Some speculate that he keeps thinking about what Mrs. Jones did for him and may now use the money she gave him to help someone else. They theorize that because he wants to say, "Thank you, m'am," he is grateful for the life lesson and the meal she provided. Others think that he is thankful for only the meal and that the life lesson hasn't registered yet but eventually will.

Next, we devote some time to physically improvising different ideas of what the behavior of Mrs. Jones and Roger might look like before the story began and after the story ended. Although we know there is no "right" way to represent either scenario, we discuss which ways seem most logical based on textual evidence and which options create visual imagery that communicates the meaning of the text.

I include here a wonderful written piece about the inner thought process of Mrs. Jones as she contemplates how to deal with Roger (see Figure 5.8). It was written by a faculty member at a professional development workshop, but articulating the inner thought process of a character can also be an excellent writing assignment for students.

> **Interior Monologue "Good Angel of Mrs. Luella Bates Washington Jones"**
> **_Luella, believe_**
>
>
> _Luella Bates Washington Jones—_
> _Look at that boy!_
> _I know, I know. He tried to snatch your purse_
> _and it could have been you all bruised up, left on the sidewalk._
>
>
> _But look at him—washing his face,_
> _trying to scrub off all that the street leave him with._
> _There's a good boy in there, a real good boy._
> _And the world don't see it so even he don't see it._
>
> _But…you see it._
>
> _Now, he just got to see it for himself._
>
> _And never no mind that Devil fool voice of yours tellin' you_
> _that boy ain't never gonna make it out._
> _Listening to that one never lead anyone to any good for too long,_
> _you know that yourself._
>
> _That boy, standing there, looking to run,_
> _that boy need somebody…somebody to believe in him._
>
> _For God's sake, Luella_
> _Believe in this boy._

**FIGURE 5.8.** Imagined interior monologue of Mrs. Luella Bates Washington Jones.


## Building Characters' Lives with Novels

Since short stories and most poems are relatively brief and concise, you can usually take readers through the three steps of the actor's process in a short period of time. You may want to apply these strategies to novels as well. Indeed, creating character biographies is an effective strategy to help readers investigate and understand complex characters, and filling in any time gaps in a novel can help readers follow the continuity of a long story. When working with novels, you can adapt any of the strategies described for "Oranges" or "Thank You, M'am." Here are some additional ideas to focus reading on the discovery of character:

1. Divide the class into groups and assign each group a character from the novel. Ask each group to trace its character's journey from the beginning of the novel to the end. Does the character change through the course of

the text? If so, what causes the character to change? If not, why not? What do you know from explicit information in the text, and what do you infer from it?

2. Assign each student a certain character for whom to write a biography.

3. Assign students to different characters from the text and ask them each to write about their character's relationship(s) with one or more other character(s). As part of this assignment, students confer with each other in character to determine their past relationships with each other.

4. Assign each student a character from the novel, as well as a student partner who is assigned a different character. Ask each pair to write about or enact a shared experience, either one described in the novel or one from their imagination.

5. Ask students to compare a character at the end of the novel with the version of that character they meet at the beginning. How does the character change, and what events in the story cause the change?

6. Ask students to improvise as characters talking to one another in situations that are described in the novel through prose rather than dialogue. How does the text inform the improvised dialogue?

7. Ask students to assume the roles of characters and talk to each other in circumstances not described in the novel.

## Building Characters' Lives in an Online Environment

The actor's reading strategies transfer easily to a remote environment. You can introduce the students to using drama and reading in the roles of actors in a synchronous virtual meeting with the whole class, then ask them to accomplish the actor's tasks of searching for and recording character evidence, extrapolating from the text to develop characters' biographies and relationships, and filling in any time gaps in the story line as individual asynchronous writing assignments. Another option would be to use your digital platform's functionality to assign students to small groups so they can talk or write collaboratively, then post their writings for others to see and compare. If students share their character biographies, accounts of character relationships, and versions of any time gaps, ask them to defend their choices to each other by justifying how they built on textual evidence to draw conclusions. This activity provides the opportunity to compare and evaluate a variety of choices.

## Wrap-Up

The actor's three reading steps—searching for and recording character evidence from the text, generating character biographies and relationships, and completing any time gaps in the story lines—give readers a way to make characters' lives concrete and visible. The steps of the actor's process ask students to partner with the text and build on evidence they find to construct the components of the characters' lives. In addition, the actor's reading strategies generate excellent writing and discussion opportunities. All of these activities, which ask students to think beyond the boundaries of the text, engage students with higher-order thinking and reasoning skills as they read.

Applying the actor's process by itself does not include any enactment, so students get to be actors without having to actually "act," which may be a relief to many. However, if you have students who want to include an enactment component, by all means add one!

# 6

# Application of the Designer's Process

## *Constructing Context*

The designer's process focuses on context and creates a concrete way for students to see what the environment of a literary work might look like. Additionally, the process asks readers to carefully examine a writer's language choices for both meaning and connotation, ultimately translating the language of the text into imagery. Since you are working with limited resources in a classroom, accept the fact that you will not be able to build an environment that reflects the underlying meaning of the literature in the way that a theatrical set designer does. Include metaphorical ideas and figurative imagery as you discuss and envision the context, but, to be practical, focus the classroom process mainly on creating an environment that accommodates the story's action.

The designer's process I describe with the mentor texts, like the actor's process, occurs over the course of two class meetings. It would be hard to condense this process into one day, as students generally need preparation time before they reconfigure the classroom to build a representation of the context of a story. In the two-day process, I use day one to introduce the concepts and accomplish the preliminary work, and we build the context in the classroom on day two.

## Students Construct Context with "Oranges"

### *Day One*

I tell the students we are going to try a new approach to reading in the next two days that will help us see what a poem's context looks like. Informing them that we will borrow some reading ideas from the world of theater, I describe, in relatively simple terms, how theater artists must read in great detail to transform literary works into stage productions. I tell them we are going to focus on the reading process of set designers, who translate language into imagery and have very specific goals when they read. A set designer must find context information within the text, envision what the story's environment looks like, and build it into reality. I assure students that we are *not* going to create stage scenery for an audience; rather, we are going to follow the set designer's reading process to find evidence of context in the text, envision what it would look like, and then create a simple representation of it in our classroom. Their curiosity is aroused, and they agree to give it a try.

I then give each student a copy of the poem "Oranges," and we all read it aloud together "as ourselves." I give them some basic information about the poem and the writer, Gary Soto, then ask if they would be willing to read the poem again but this time engage in a little role-playing with me. I tell them we will all now read as set designers who will create an environment for the poem, and I will participate as an executive designer helping them to achieve their goals as designers. Our three reading goals as designers will be as follows:

Step 1. Search for and record evidence of context from the text.

Step 2. Visualize the context in the classroom.

Step 3. Create a representation of the context in the classroom.

I distribute the designer's worklist and ask the students if they are ready to read the poem again.

> **The Designer's Worklist**
>
> **A.** Search the text to find and record the following information:
>
> > **1.** Where does the action take place? Does it occur in more than one location?
> >
> > **2.** If characters move from one location to another, what are the requirements, if any, for space between the locations?
> >
> > **3.** What is the time period? Past? Present? Future?
> >
> > **4.** At what time(s) of day does the action occur?
> >
> > **5.** What is the season?
> >
> > **6.** How can our classroom be rearranged to represent the location(s) of the text?
> >
> > **7.** What does the environment need to include (e.g., walkways, walls, doors, windows, stairways, furniture, props) to accommodate the action of the text?
>
> **B.** Using the available space and furniture, visualize the text's environment in the classroom.
>
> **C.** Determine how the environment will accommodate the action of the text.

D. Draw a sketch of how you envision reconfiguring the classroom to create the text's environment.

E. Create a representation of the context in the classroom.

We now begin our reading as set designers.

### Step 1: Search for and Record Evidence of Context from the Text

I remind students that as they read as designers, they must record evidence of context that they find, and I give them multiple options for recording evidence from the text (see Figures 6.1 and 6.2). Some write directly on copies of the text, identifying context evidence by underlining or circling words and writing notes; some take notes on laptops or tablets; others do so with pen and paper; and some record evidence on worksheets (available in the appendix). All of these methods provide effective ways for readers to record evidence of context, so choose the note-taking technique that you think will be most efficient for your students, or give them options and let them choose. Students can search for context information individually or in groups.

I ask these students to work individually. I give them fifteen minutes to find context evidence, and then we have a collective discussion about what they find.

#### WHAT THEY FIND

Using the questions I gave them, students discover an abundance of context evidence in the text of "Oranges":

1. *Where does the action take place? Does it occur in more than one location?*

   They find evidence of three major locations:

   a. The girl's house ("As I walked toward / Her house")

   b. The drugstore ("we were breathing / Before a drugstore. We / Entered")

   c. Path between the girl's house and the drugstore ("led / Her down the street" and "I took my girl's hand / in mine for two blocks")

2. *If characters move from one location to another, what are the requirements, if any, for space between the locations?*

   Students find evidence that the characters walk from the girl's house to the drugstore and then from the drugstore back to her house or to another place ("led / Her down the street" and "Outside, / A few cars hissing past, / Fog hanging like old / Coats between the trees. I took my girl's hand / in mine for two blocks").

# Oranges

By Gary Soto

*annotation: props*

The first time I walked
With a girl, I was twelve,
Cold, and weighted down
With two oranges in my jacket. *— clothing prop*
5  December. Frost cracking *— season: winter*
Beneath my steps, my breath
Before me, then gone.
As I walked toward *→ setting: neighborhood*
Her house, the one whose
10  Porch light burned yellow
Night and day, in any weather.
A dog barked at me, until *scenery*
She came out pulling
At her gloves, face bright *— clothing prop*
15  With rouge. I smiled,
Touched her shoulder, and led
Her down the street, across *— location: outside*
A used car lot and a line
Of newly planted trees,
20  Until we were breathing
Before a drugstore. We
Entered, the tiny bell
Bringing a saleslady
Down a narrow aisle of goods.
25  I turned to the candies
Tiered like bleachers,
And asked what she wanted—
Light in her eyes, a smile
Starting at the corners
30  Of her mouth. I fingered
A nickel in my pocket, *— prop*
And when she lifted a chocolate *— prop*
That cost a dime,
I didn't say anything.
35  I took the nickel from
My pocket, then an orange, *— props*
And set them quietly on
The counter. When I looked up,
The lady's eyes met mine,
40  And held them, knowing
Very well what it was all
About.
    Outside
A few cars hissing past,
Fog hanging like old *— setting/location: outside street, sidewalk?*
45  Coats between the trees.
I took my girl's hand
In mine for two blocks,
Then released it to let
Her unwrap the chocolate.
50  I peeled my orange
That was so bright against
The gray of December *— season: winter*
That, from a distance,
Someone might have thought
55  I was making a fire in my hands.

*annotations in margin:* time of year; clothing prop; time era: not modern day; location; time era: only ten cents

**FIGURE 6.1.** Notes about context evidence found in the text.

68    APPLICATION IN THE CLASSROOM

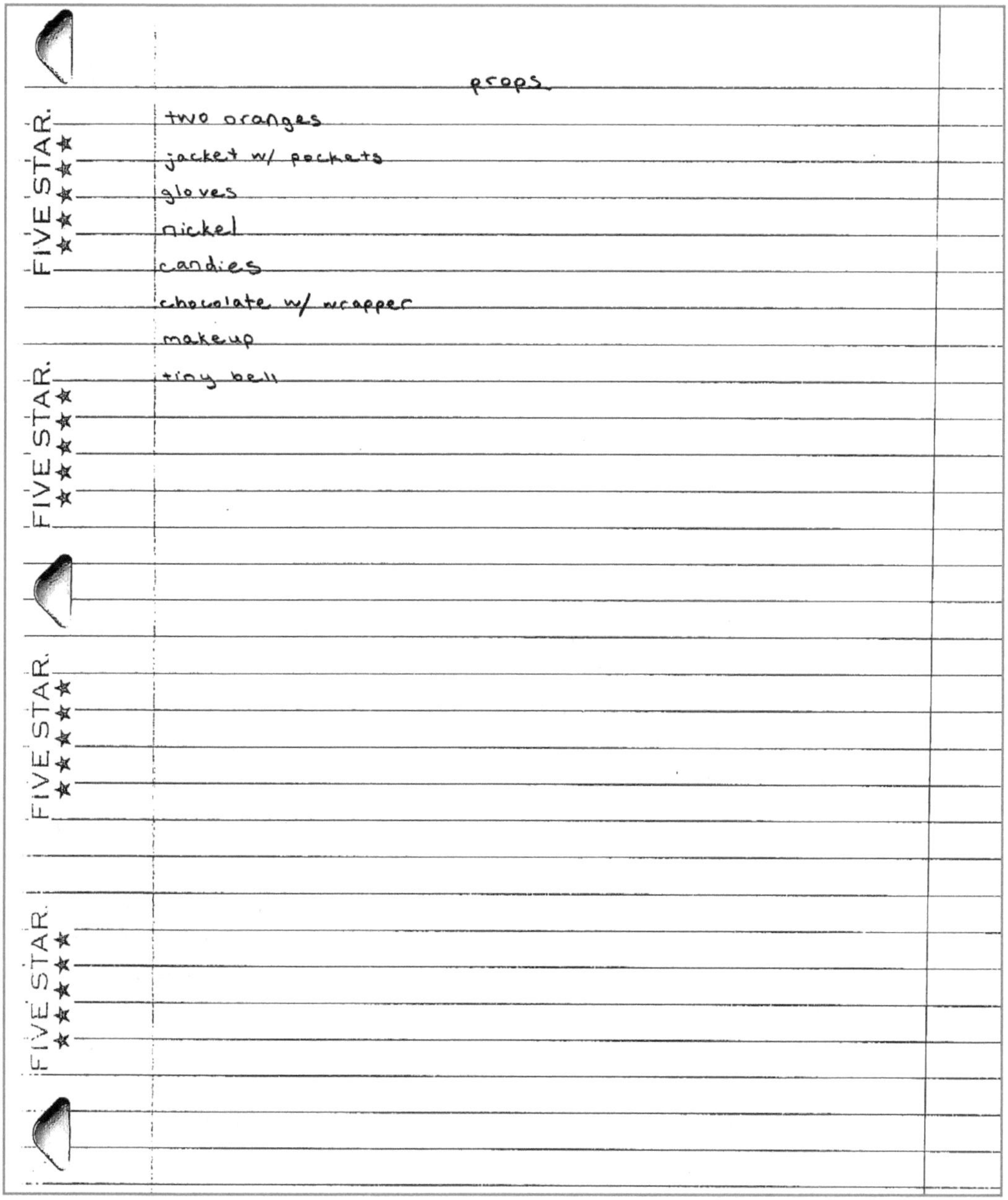
props

two oranges
jacket w/ pockets
gloves
nickel
candies
chocolate w/ wrapper
makeup
tiny bell

**FIGURE 6.2.** Prop list.

3. *What is the time period? Past? Present? Future?*

   Students discover it is the past because the chocolate candy cost only ten cents ("she lifted a chocolate / That cost a dime"). They also think the use of the term *drugstore* is from a previous era.

4. *At what time(s) of day does the action occur?*

   The text does not specify a time, so here students must begin to make inferences. Most think the action occurs during the afternoon, though some think perhaps evening since the porch light is on; on rereading the text, however, they discover that the porch light always burned ("the one whose / Porch light burned yellow / Night and day"). Students also think that since this is "The first time [the narrator] walked / With a girl," it would more likely be in the afternoon than in the evening. They think the phrase "Fog hanging like old / Coats between the trees" indicates that it might be later in the afternoon, when fog comes in.

5. *What is the season?*

   The text says "December," and students determine that it is cold: "Frost cracking / Beneath my steps, my breath / Before me, then gone" and "She came out pulling / At her gloves."

6. *How can our classroom be rearranged to represent the location(s) of the text?*

   Students decide that they need a space for the girl's house, a space for the drugstore, and a walkway on which the girl and the narrator can walk between those two locations. The saleslady also needs a walking space in order to approach the counter in the drugstore. Students think we can use two corners of the room as the girl's house and the drugstore, respectively, and clear a path between them for the narrator and the girl to walk.

7. *What does the environment need to include (e.g., walkways, walls, doors, windows, stairways, furniture, props) to accommodate the action of the text?*

   The environment needs a pathway from the girl's house to the drugstore ("led / Her down the street, across / A used car lot and a line / Of newly planted trees, / Until we were breathing / Before a drugstore"). The saleslady comes from somewhere else in the store to the counter, and a bell needs to ring when the narrator and the girl walk into the store ("We / Entered, the tiny bell / Bringing a saleslady / Down a narrow aisle of goods"). There also needs to be a display of candies "Tiered like bleachers." The environment also needs the following furniture and props:

   Drugstore counter ("And set them quietly on / The counter")
   Candy display ("the candies / Tiered like bleachers")
   Two oranges ("two oranges in my jacket")
   Jacket ("two oranges in my jacket")
   Gloves ("She came out pulling / At her gloves")
   Bell ("the tiny bell / Bringing a saleslady")
   Nickel ("I fingered / A nickel in my pocket")

## Step 2: Visualize the Context in the Classroom

Once students find and record the evidence of context, their next task is to visualize what the space would look like in the classroom. This visualization step can be done either individually or in collaborative groups. I divide the class into three groups and ask each group to envision the context of "Oranges" in the classroom. This approach creates an opportunity for collaboration and provides a chance to compare ideas. I give the groups fifteen minutes to talk among themselves, write a description, and draw a rough sketch of their idea (see Figure 6.3). I ask them to choose one member of the group to explain their vision to the rest of the class.

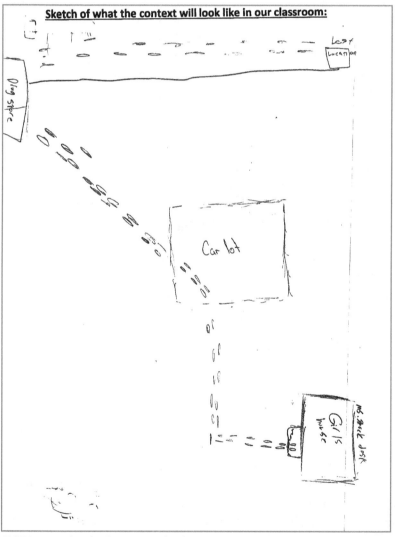

**FIGURE 6.3.** Sketch of a group's idea for context in the classroom.

## What They Envision

The groups see the context for "Oranges" in their classroom in three different configurations. I ask them to use language from the text to justify their ideas.

### Group 1

Put the girl's house in one corner of the room and the drugstore in another corner, where the teacher's desk is. Create the walkway ("across / A used car lot and the line / Of newly planted trees") along the wall between the two corners. Use the teacher's desk as the counter and put the candies on it. Make a hallway in the drugstore along another wall, with the saleslady in a back room so she can come "Down a narrow aisle of goods" when she hears the bell on the door. After leaving, the girl and the narrator go back to the girl's house on the same path they used in coming to the drugstore. We want a bench (two chairs) along the wall for them to sit on as she eats the chocolate and the narrator peels the orange. The text does not mention a bench, but we like the idea of the girl sitting down to unwrap her candy and the narrator sitting next to her peeling the orange.

### Group 2

The girl's house is at the door to the classroom, and the girl is outside of the room until "She [comes] out pulling / At her gloves." The two characters walk diagonally across the room ("across / A used car lot and the line / Of newly planted trees") toward the drugstore, which is at the room's diagonally opposite corner. Use a chair to represent the door into the drugstore and tie a bell to it so that it will ring when they open the door, "Bringing a saleslady / Down a narrow aisle of goods." The girl and the narrator walk back toward her house the same way they came and stop near her house to eat the candy and the orange.

### Group 3

Have the girl's house at the far corner of the room and the drugstore on the opposite wall by the windows. Use the bookshelf for the drugstore counter and the windowsill to display the "candies / Tiered like bleachers." The saleslady comes "Down a narrow aisle of goods" along the window and goes behind the bookshelf. Make sure the bookshelf is set so that the action ("I took the nickel from / My pocket, then an orange, / And set them quietly on / The counter. When I looked up, / The lady's eyes met mine, / And held them, knowing / Very well what it was all / About") can be easily seen since it is important to the story. The narrator and the girl walk a different way when they leave the drugstore, along another wall to a place where they stop to eat the chocolate and the orange.

After hearing from each group, I remind the readers again that there is no "right" way to represent the context. Still, we will have to make some decisions because we can build only one environment in the classroom. I tell them their homework is to consider all of the ideas they heard today, from their own group and the other groups, and think about the best way to represent the environment of "Oranges" in our classroom. We will tackle the building process tomorrow.

## Day Two

## Step 2: Visualize the Context in the Classroom

### DELVING DEEPER: FINDING MORE MEANING

At this point in the process, you will need to put on your executive designer hat and guide the students to decide on one design to build. If you don't, you will never get past this stage! You cannot create every option they envision, so take the lead and guide them to determine the most effective representation of the context and make a choice about what to create in the classroom.

With my executive designer hat on, I remind the students that there is no "right" way to represent the environment of "Oranges" in the classroom, then lead them in a focused discussion of the many insights they have developed about the context from their search for evidence. We compare as many of their ideas as possible, including ideas about the poem's meaning, but we focus on the decision-making process and on making a choice that is the most practical and can best accommodate the story's action. Asking students to discuss options and make decisions requires them to continually refer back to textual evidence to justify their inferences and conclusions.

With my guidance, we choose to place the girl's house at the classroom entrance since there's already a door there, and we place the drugstore at the diagonally opposite corner of the room with a pathway across the middle of the room between the two locations. We decide on this configuration because it will give us the most space as the narrator leads "her down the street, across / A used car lot and a line / Of newly planted trees" until they reach the drugstore. The teacher's desk in the corner gives us a nice surface for the drugstore counter ("I took the nickel from / My pocket, then an orange, / And set them quietly on / The counter"). We also agree to place a student desk next to the teacher's desk for the candy display ("the candies / Tiered like bleachers"). We decide to place the saleslady in a back room of the drugstore along another wall of the classroom ("Bringing a saleslady / Down a narrow aisle of goods"). We also agree to give the girl and the narrator a walking path along a different wall of the classroom when they leave the drugstore and walk for two blocks ("Outside, / A few cars hissing past, / Fog hanging like old / Coats between the trees").

As we make decisions about the elements of the design we will create, we reread parts of the text to verify that all of our choices will result in a context that supports the text and accommodates its action. We are now ready to create the environment, and we draw a sketch of the design we have chosen.

## Step 3. Create a Representation of the Context in the Classroom

### RECONFIGURING THE CLASSROOM

The process of rearranging your classroom, disrupting your ordered world, and building the context of a literary work into reality can be both challenging and disconcerting. Take a deep breath before you begin this step and remind yourself that transforming your students' ideas into reality validates their creative thinking and gives them a concrete way to see what they are reading. Remember too that your classroom will be returned to its normal order when the process is over. Be sure to leave time to do this.

We decide that since the door to the room is already there, the girl can be outside and come in through the door "pulling / At her gloves" when the narrator arrives. To create the space for the narrator and the girl to walk "down the street, across / A used car lot and a line / Of newly planted trees," we move desks to open up an area across the center of the room. Referring back to the text and reminding ourselves that the saleslady is not at the counter when the narrator and the girl arrive, we move a small bookcase from along the wall to give her a "back room" and enough space to come "Down a narrow aisle of goods" when she hears the bell. To accommodate the bell, we place a chair near the desk to serve as the door to the drugstore and decide to attach the bell to it on a string so that it will ring when the door is "opened" or "closed."

We also place a student desk next to the teacher's desk for the candy display and decide that the teacher's desk can stay where it is to serve as the drugstore counter. We make sure there is enough room in front of the counter for the narrator and enough room behind it for the saleslady, and we clear a space on the desk where the narrator can put the nickel and the orange ("I took the nickel from / My pocket, then an orange, / And set them quietly on / The counter"). To give the narrator and the girl a different walking route when they leave the drugstore, we create a pathway from the drugstore to another corner of the classroom by moving a few more desks. We also clear a destination space, where the girl can "unwrap the chocolate" while the narrator peels the orange.

Once we have rearranged the classroom, I give the designers a bag of props that I have brought in—an assortment of items needed for the poem's action. I often provide the props for this process to give the students a special surprise when we get to this stage. The bag contains two oranges, a jacket, a pair of gloves, a bell, a small bag of assorted candies (including some chocolates), and a nickel, all of which I found in my house. I ask students to refer back to the text and place the props where they belong in the environment. With some string we find in

the classroom, they attach the bell to the chair that is the drugstore "door." Students also find several tissue boxes in the classroom and arrange them on the bookshelf so that the candy display can be "Tiered like bleachers." They place the gloves outside the classroom door for the girl and put the oranges and the nickel in the pockets of the jacket for the narrator.

When the environment is built and the props are placed, we read the poem aloud again and envision the action occurring in the setting we have created. We agree that the environment we have built will accommodate the action of the poem, and we are pleased with what we have accomplished. If you have time, and if you and your students are so inclined, you can choose several students to take on the roles of actors and walk through the story in character to verify that the environment you have built will accommodate the action.

I always make sure to leave enough time at the end of the class to restore the classroom to its original configuration and return all of the props to the bag. Once the students are settled again, I give them a homework assignment: Describe how searching for evidence of context, envisioning the context, and actually building the environment in the classroom helped you understand Gary Soto's poem "Oranges."

# Students Construct Context with "Thank You, M'am"

## Day One

I begin the designer's process with the usual front-loading by letting students know that we will be doing something different with reading during the next two days. Telling them that we are going to borrow ideas from the world of the theater, I describe how theater artists must read with great precision and accuracy in order to transform literary works into stage productions. I explain that we are going to focus on the reading process of a set designer, who envisions and creates the context of a story. I note that when set designers read, they must look for and find very specific context information in the text, then use that information along with their imagination to transform the language of the text into imagery. They must envision what the environment will look like, how it can accommodate the action of the story, and how it can be built for the stage.

I then give each student a copy of "Thank You, M'am," provide some background on the story and on writer Langston Hughes, and we read the story aloud together "as ourselves." Afterward, I tell students that we are now going to read the story again, but this time we will engage in a little role-playing and read the story as set designers while I play the role of executive designer to help them achieve their reading goals. Some trepidation creeps across the room, but ultimately the students think this is an interesting challenge and agree to give it a try. I tell them that as we read, we will work toward the following three goals:

Step 1. Search for and record evidence of context from the text.

Step 2. Visualize the context in the classroom.

Step 3. Create a representation of the context in the classroom.

I give students the designer's worklist (the same as for "Oranges"), specifying what they need to accomplish as they read as set designers, and we review it. We then begin our reading work as designers.

### Step 1: Search for and Record Evidence of Context from the Text

I let students choose their method of note-taking. Some write directly on the text, some take notes on laptops, some write notes on paper, and others use worksheets (see Figure 6.4). I ask this particular class to work individually rather than in groups as they search the text to find answers to the questions, and I give them fifteen minutes. They find substantial information about context as they reread the text of "Thank You, M'am" as designers.

## WHAT THEY FIND

1.  *Where does the action take place? Does it occur in more than one location?*

    Students identify three locations in the story from textual references:

    a. A sidewalk ("the boy fell on his back on the sidewalk")

    b. A street to walk on ("the large woman, starting up the street, dragging the frightened boy behind her")

    c. Mrs. Jones's living space ("she dragged the boy inside, down a hall, and into a large kitchenette-furnished room at the rear of the house")

| WORSHEET 1: | |
|---|---|
| Literary Work: Thank You Ma'am | |
| Set Designer(s): Kathryn, Ysabella, Shreya, Sofia, M, Sofia S., Dhilan, Joaquin, Shakur, Jaden, Isabella, Kate S. | |
| Number of Locations | 3 |
| Define Location(s) | ① Ally where she turns a corner ② Streets ③ Daybed / living space |
| Time era references<br><br>1950's | ① Ice box ② Pocketbook ③ Blue suede shows ($10) ④ 10¢ cake |
| Time(s) of Day/Night<br>Season | ① Summer 11:00pm |
| Reflection of Characters in the environment ① Woman at first is angry. ② Then she asks boy questions ③ Understanding/empathetic | ① First boy is confused and desperate ② Then boy is embarassed ③ Wants to earn trust still intimidated ④ Grateful |

**FIGURE 6.4.** Worksheet for recording evidence of context.

2. *If characters move from one location to another, what are the requirements, if any, for space between the locations?*

   The characters do walk from one location to another. Actually, Mrs. Jones drags Roger ("dragging the frightened boy behind her") to her boarding-house. We need enough space to accommodate the time it takes for the characters' conversation.

3. *What is the time period? Past? Present? Future?*

   Students find text references indicating an era from the past: "blue suede shoes," "ten-cent cake," "icebox."

4. *At what time(s) of day does the action occur?*

   The text tells students specifically: "It was about eleven o'clock at night, dark."

5. *What is the season?*

   Students find no direct mention of a season and therefore begin to make inferences from the text. They conclude that the weather is warm since much of the action takes place outside and there is no mention of a coat for either character. Also, when the characters arrive at Mrs. Jones's house, she leaves "the door open."

6. *How can our classroom be rearranged to represent the location(s) of the text?*

   These particular students meet in an exceptionally large classroom that includes a space with moveable desks, an area with high-top tables and stools, and a carpeted reading area with couches and bookshelves. They decide they can clear a space among the desks to create the street where the two characters meet, have the characters move between the tables as Mrs. Jones drags Roger to her boardinghouse, and use the reading area as her furnished room.

7. *What does the environment need to include (e.g., walkways, walls, doors, windows, stairways, furniture, props) to accommodate the action of the text?*

   Students determine that there needs to be an open space for the initial action in the street with significant distance for the characters to make the walk from the street corner to the boardinghouse since substantial dialogue occurs as Mrs. Jones takes Roger to her house. They also determine that the furniture in the boardinghouse room should be arranged so that Roger can see the door from the sink ("Roger looked at the door—looked at the woman—looked at the door—*and went to the sink*") and that there needs to be a place for Roger to sit where Mrs. Jones can see him when she goes behind the screen ("the boy took care to sit on the far side of the room, away from the purse, where he thought she could easily see him out of the corner of her eye if she wanted to"). The environment also needs the following furniture and props:

> A large purse with a strap that breaks ("a large purse that had everything in it but a hammer and nails. It had a long strap. . . . The strap broke with the sudden single tug the boy gave it from behind")
>
> In Mrs. Jones's boardinghouse room: sink, daybed, table, two chairs, screen, stove, icebox, and shelves to hold things in the kitchen area
>
> Comb ("You might run that comb through your hair")
>
> Washcloth ("you go to that sink and wash your face")
>
> Towel ("Here's a clean towel")
>
> Money ("Now here, take this ten dollars and buy yourself some blue suede shoes")
>
> Ham, lima beans, cocoa ("She heated some lima beans and ham . . . made the cocoa")
>
> Cake and knife ("she cut him a half of her ten-cent cake")
>
> Cups, plates, silverware, napkins ("set the table")

## Step 2: Visualize the Context in the Classroom

I then ask students to work in three groups to envision the environment of "Thank You, M'am." Since their specific classroom is so large and accommodating for this kind of work, they verify their initial idea for the space and unanimously concur on the environment. They agree that they can move desks to create an open area for the initial meeting of the two characters, then have them walk between and around the high-top tables to get to the boardinghouse. They love the idea of using the carpeted reading area as Mrs. Jones's room in the boardinghouse.

A more conventional classroom can also be reconfigured to accommodate this story with a little more imagination. In the next two chapters, "Application of the Director's Process" and "Application of the Collaborative Process," you will find descriptions of how students configured a more conventional classroom to represent the environment of "Thank you, M'am."

### DECIDING ON A DESIGN

If you have differing ideas for the arrangement of the setting in a more conventional classroom space, put on your executive designer hat. Guide your students through a discussion of the insights discovered about the context from the search for evidence, then direct them toward choosing the most effective and practical design to accommodate the action of the story. I don't have to do that with this class because they are unanimous in their thoughts about how to use the classroom space to create the story's environment. We draw a sketch of how we want to use the space before we leave for the day (see Figure 6.5).

**FIGURE 6.5.** Sketch of the context for "Thank You, M'am."

## Day Two

### Step 3: Create a Representation of the Context in the Classroom

#### RECONFIGURING THE CLASSROOM

This group of students takes the initiative with this process. Of course, this aspect will vary with each class. Be sure to maintain your role of executive designer throughout the process of rearranging the classroom so that you can help mediate differences of opinion, ensure the creation of one cohesive and practical design, and keep students on task.

#### DELVING DEEPER: FINDING MORE MEANING

To create the environment for "Thank You, M'am," students begin by moving some of the desks to create an open space where Roger can confront Mrs. Jones on the street corner. They move the stools out of the way so that Mrs. Jones can drag Roger between the high-top tables toward her boardinghouse. They think that this route will provide enough space and time for the conversation that occurs between the two characters during their journey from the street corner to her house. Using the carpeted area to represent Mrs. Jones's room in the board-inghouse, they designate locations for two doors, one into the boardinghouse and another into her room, then refer back to the text and their notes to confirm what furniture and props need to be in her room. They realize the interior of her room needs a daybed, a table with two chairs, and a sink, and a kitchenette area with a gas plate and an icebox. They refer back to the text multiple times to make sure they have included everything the text has specified.

I remind them at this point that the room needs to be arranged so that it accommodates the action of the story. They once again consult the text and their notes, then place the table so that Mrs. Jones can still see Roger out of the cor-ner of her eye when she is behind the screen in the kitchen area ("the boy took care to sit on the far side of the room, away from the purse, where he thought she could easily see him out of the corner of her eye"). A couple of the students move into the spaces to see if Mrs. Jones can see Roger out of the corner of her eye. She can! Actually creating the physical arrangement and the action that occurs within it helps students develop a much clearer perception of how Mrs. Jones and Roger interact in the space.

They continue to move furniture around in the carpeted area and place a small table inside the kitchenette area for the icebox and the gas plate. As they wonder how to represent the screen that partitions off the kitchenette area ("In another corner of the room behind a screen was a gas plate and an icebox"), I suggest using the open bookshelf that stands against the wall. They determine that the shelf can also serve as a place to store the cups, plates, silverware, napkins, ham, lima beans, and ten-cent cake needed in the story.

I now present students with the bag of props I have brought in, which contains a purse with a long strap, a comb, a towel, a washcloth, a dollar bill to represent the ten-dollar bill, and a pitcher for the cocoa. Since I didn't see the need to actually cook a ham and lima beans or bake a cake for this class exercise, I used a small bag of pretzels to represent the ham and lima beans and a chocolate fiber bar for the cake. I also included some plates, napkins, cups, silverware, and a few bowls—all of which I had scrounged from around my house. As I give the

students the bag of props, I tell them to place each one where it belongs in the environment. Referring back to the text, they place a bowl on top of a box for a sink and set the towel, washcloth, and comb nearby. They move the open bookshelf to represent the "screen" that separates the room from the kitchenette and place the plates, cups, napkins, silverware, and food on the shelf unit. As they are physically positioning all of this furniture and arranging the props, several of the students comment about how cramped Mrs. Jones's boardinghouse space is—something they had not envisioned while reading the text. We also discuss how her cramped living situation reflects that she is not a wealthy woman.

Once we have reconfigured the space as a representation of the environment of "Thank You, M'am," we reread the story to visualize whether it will accommodate the action of the story. A couple of the students want to enact the characters, so I let them walk through a simple version of the action as we read, and we are all pleased at how well our environment enables us to tell the story. Several students remark that when reading the story, they had not grasped all the details of the space, but building the environment has given them a way to see the context and the action within it.

I am always conscious of leaving enough time at the end of the class session for the students to restore all of the furniture to its original place in the room and to retrieve all of the props. As they do this, they congratulate themselves on their good work.

I ask them to write a one-page essay as homework: How did creating the environment in the classroom help you understand "Thank You, M'am"?

## Creating Context with Novels

Creating the context of a whole novel can be difficult since novels often span long time frames and occur in multiple locations. However, any of the strategies of the designer's process—from focused reading to visualizing a space to constructing an environment in the classroom—can be used to illuminate specific scenes or portions of a novel. In other words, any of the strategies used for "Oranges" or "Thank You, M'am" can be adapted for use with novels.

Here are some additional ways to use the designer's process to gear reading toward the discovery of context and help readers see the context of a novel:

1. Divide the class into small groups and assign each group a specific location within the novel. Ask each group to construct, draw, or describe what

their specific location looks like. Ask each group to justify what they have created based on textual references.

2. As a whole class, in groups, or individually, ask students to discuss how characters move from one location in the story to another. Compare ideas and the textual references on which they are based.

3. Make a list of the main props or artifacts in a specific chapter or scene. Then discuss why they are important to that part of the novel and how they contribute to the meaning of the whole story.

4. Determine how the time period of the novel is reflected in the environment. Divide the class into groups and ask each group of readers to find references about the time period in different chapters or parts of the novel.

## Creating Context in an Online Environment

Students can search the text and record evidence of context in an online environment, but it is not practical to ask them to envision and build the environment in a classroom that doesn't exist in physical space. Consequently, when implementing the designer's process remotely, you must think about creating context a little differently. Still, it certainly can be done.

You can orient your students to drama and to the designer's reading process in a synchronous session with the whole class, then allow them to work individually or, if possible, use your computer platform's capacity to break students into small groups to work collaboratively to find context information in the text. They can then extrapolate from the textual content and share ideas about what the environment might look like.

Theater designers use any of numerous computer programs to render drawings of their designs, but these apps are costly, complex, and unnecessary for our reading process. Fortunately, you can find very simple apps that allow students to create a space, populate it with furniture, and move characters around in it. Of course, students can always draw a simple sketch of what a story's environment might look like with good old paper and pencil. While you won't be able to rearrange actual furniture in a virtual classroom (and some teachers will be thrilled by this fact), you can still give students the opportunity to find context information in a text and visualize how the story's environment might be translated into space.

## Wrap-Up

For students who have trouble visualizing what they read, the designer's process helps them create a concrete construction of a story's environment that they can see and move around in. The process of searching the text to find and record evidence of context, envisioning what it might look like, and creating a representation of it in the classroom shows students how to closely examine the writer's words and translate them into both symbolic and physical imagery. Within that context, the process also facilitates students' ability to see the story's action. Repeated application of this process will help students discover both the practical and the metaphorical aspects of a story's context as they learn to construct the environment in their mind while reading.

# 7

# Application of the Director's Process

## *Generating Action*

T he director's process can be a challenge to apply on its own because the director's work is so interconnected with the work of the actor and the designer. However, with its focus on action, the director's process is especially valuable to reading comprehension, as it challenges students not only to uncover a story's action but also to verify its causality and determine how to represent it. If you choose to focus on the director's process, plan to include parts of both the designer's process and the actor's process in your instruction as well. I will describe how I do so in this chapter.

As with the actor's and designer's processes, I will use the two mentor texts and take you through a two-day application of the director's process. If you wish to explore the literature in more depth, you can definitely spend more than two days with this process.

## Students Generate Action with "Oranges"

### *Day One*

As with the other artists' processes, I begin by telling students that today and tomorrow we will be doing something very different and challenging with reading. Informing them we are going to borrow some reading strategies from the theater—and especially from stage directors—I describe how theater artists must read in a special and detailed way to transform literary works into stage productions. I tell them that one of the director's main goals in a stage production is to identify and create a story's action. In order to do so, the director must not only read closely to discover *what* the action is but also add their imagination to the text to determine *how* the action will be represented on the stage.

I inform students that we are going to read a poem once "as ourselves," then read it again as directors by applying the three steps of the director's reading process:

1. Search for and record evidence of physical and verbal action from the text.

2. Conceptualize the physical and verbal action.

3. Transform the action into concrete reality.

I tell them that they will receive a worklist specifying their reading tasks as directors and that I will serve as the executive director to guide them toward their goals.

I sense that they are somewhat intimidated, but they agree to go along.

I give each student a copy of "Oranges," we read it aloud together as ourselves, and I give students some background on the poem and the writer. I then ask if they would be willing to read the poem again but this time engage in a little role-playing with me. I tell them we are all now going to read the poem as directors who read to find, record, envision, and create the poem's physical and verbal action. I then give each student a copy of the director's worklist.

---

**The Director's Worklist**

**A.** Identify the sequence of physical and verbal actions that tell the story from beginning to end.

   **1.** What is the sequence of actions that takes the characters from the beginning of the text to the end? (Look specifically for action verbs and underline them.)

   **2.** Revisit your list of actions, this time from the last action to the first. Has each action been motivated by the previous one, thus verifying the continuity of the text?

   **3.** What does each character's voice sound like?

   **4.** What is happening during any pauses?

**B.** How can our classroom be rearranged to represent the location(s) of the text? What needs to be in the environment to accommodate the action of the text? What furniture and props are needed? Sketch out a rough drawing of the environment.

**C.** Construct the environment in the classroom and transform the action into concrete reality in the environment.

---

We begin our reading as directors.

## Step 1: Search for and Record Evidence of Physical and Verbal Action from the Text

As students begin their search for evidence of action in the text, guided by the director's worklist, I make sure they know the distinction between physical and verbal action. I also remind them that they must record what they find, and I give them the option to write on the text, take notes separately, or use a worksheet (see Figures 7.1 and 7.2). I point out that questions concerning the poem's context are included in their worklist and explain that, since they are not working with designers, they must also envision and create a space in which the action can occur.

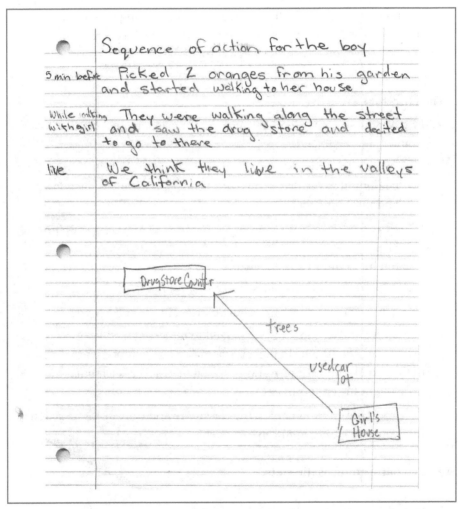

**FIGURE 7.1.** Beginning to create a list of actions as well as ideas for a space in which they can occur.

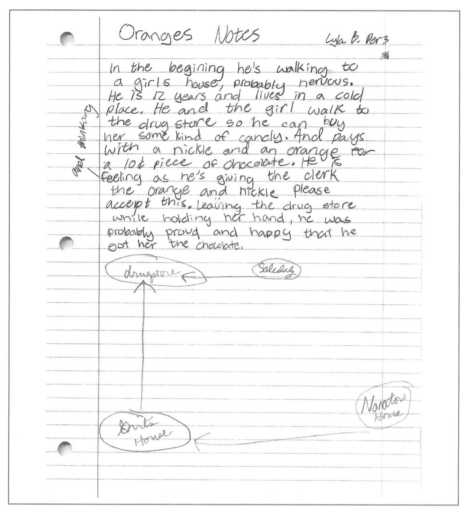

**FIGURE 7.2.** Writing out actions in paragraph form and sketching a possible arrangement for the environment.

I place the students in groups of three so they can share ideas, and I give them fifteen minutes to accomplish the task of finding evidence of action in the text. This approach provides the opportunity to compare their identified sequences of action, vocal characteristics, and ideas for representing the environment in the classroom.

## WHAT THEY FIND

1. *What is the sequence of actions that takes the characters from the beginning of the text to the end? (Look specifically for action verbs and <u>underline</u> them.)*

Students identify a distinct sequence of actions specified by the writer and underline the action verbs. The actions in this poem are easily identified, and the lists of actions created by the various groups are virtually the same.

   a. The narrator <u>walks</u> to the girl's house ("as I walked toward / Her house").

   b. They <u>walk</u> together to the drugstore ("and led / Her down the street, across / A used car lot and a line / Of newly planted trees, / Until we were breathing / Before a drugstore").

   c. They <u>enter</u> the drugstore ("We / Entered").

   d. The narrator <u>looks</u> at the candies ("I turned to the candies").

   e. The narrator <u>asks</u> her what she wants ("asked her what she wanted").

   f. The girl <u>makes her decision</u> about the candy ("she lifted a chocolate / That cost a dime").

   g. The narrator <u>makes a decision</u> and <u>places</u> a nickel and an orange on the counter to pay for the chocolate ("I didn't say anything. / I took the nickel from / My pocket, then an orange, / And set them quietly on / The counter").

   h. The saleslady and the narrator <u>look</u> at each other ("When I looked up, / The lady's eyes met mine, / And held them, knowing / Very well what it was all / About"), and the saleslady <u>accepts</u> the nickel and the orange as payment for the candy.

   i. The narrator and the girl <u>go</u> outside ("Outside, / A few cars hissing past").

   j. They <u>hold hands and walk</u> two blocks ("I took my girl's hand / In mine for two blocks").

   k. The narrator <u>releases</u> the girl's hand, and she <u>unwraps</u> the chocolate as the narrator <u>peels</u> the remaining orange ("Then released it to let / Her unwrap the chocolate. / I peeled my orange").

As students create this list of actions, they realize the importance of the verbs to the action. They note that their list is made up of action verbs such as *walk, enter, look,* and *stop*.

2. *Revisit your list of actions, this time from the last action to the first. Has each action been motivated by the previous one, thus verifying the continuity of the text?*

   Students start at the end of the sequence of actions and verify that each action has been motivated by the previous one.

3. *What does each character's voice sound like?*

   Students discover that most of the action in the poem occurs without dialogue. They decide on the following characteristics (or lack thereof!):

   Narrator—nervous, hesitant, but trying to sound confident

   Girl—never heard

   Saleslady—never heard

4. *What is happening during any pauses?*

   After the girl selects the chocolate and puts it on the counter, a lot happens between the narrator and the saleslady. Lacking sufficient money to pay for the chocolate, the narrator has to decide what action to take. Once the narrator puts the nickel and the orange on the counter, the saleslady has to decide what action to take. The narrator and the saleslady look at each other and come to an agreement.

   When the narrator and the girl have walked two blocks, they each think about whether they like each other.

## Step 2: Conceptualize the Physical and Verbal Action

To complete the next steps of the process—conceptualization and enactment—the directors must create an environment for the action. I include questions about the context in the director's worklist so that as students search for evidence of action, they are thinking about an environment for the action as well.

At this point, you must put on your executive designer's hat and coach the directors through a mini version of the designer's process. I tell them that they are receiving a special bonus because they will learn how to read not only as directors but also as designers! (To refresh your memory about the designer's process, review Chapter 2, "Reading as a Designer.")

I give the directors five minutes to confer again, in their same groups, in order to review their answers to questions B and C on the worklist. Each group then shares its vision of the environment in the classroom. As executive designer, I now conduct a discussion to focus students' ideas and suggestions, and we decide on one option to build in the classroom. Remember, there is no "right" way to represent the environment. Always guide students to justify their decisions with evidence from the text, and while you will discuss various ways in which the meaning of the literature could be reflected in the context, focus the building process toward making choices that will accommodate the story's action in a practical manner.

We decide to place the girl's house in one corner of the room and the drugstore at an adjacent corner so that the characters can walk along the wall to get between the two locations. Students think this setup will give the narrator enough space for the indicated action ("and led / Her down the street, across / A used car lot and a line / Of newly planted trees"). I ask what is needed in the drugstore, and, referring back to the text again, they agree that they need a counter ("set them quietly on / The counter") and a candy display ("candies / Tiered like bleachers"). I ask where the narrator and the girl go when they exit the drugstore, and students decide that the narrator walks the girl home ("I took my girl's hand / in mine for two blocks"), so they can retrace their steps back to the girl's house, eating the candy and peeling the orange along the way ("to let / Her unwrap the chocolate. / I peeled my orange").

Once students decide on this option for the environment, they draw a sketch of it so that they will remember it for tomorrow when we actually build it and enact the poem's sequence of actions.

## Day Two

### Constructing the Context

As we begin day two, our first task is to construct the environment so that we can accomplish the director's third step of transforming the action into concrete reality. We work today as a whole team of directors instead of splitting into groups. We get out yesterday's sketch of the environment and, as a whole class, rearrange the classroom furniture to construct the environment we decided on yesterday. We move some desks away from the wall to give the narrator and the girl enough space to walk, and we place a bookshelf in the corner of the room to represent the drugstore counter and candy display.

I now hand the directors the bag of props I have brought in—which includes two oranges, a jacket, a pair of gloves, a bell, some candy (including a chocolate), and a nickel—and ask them to distribute the props where they belong in the environment. Students place the two oranges and the nickel in the jacket pocket and hold it for the narrator. They place the gloves at the girl's house and the candies on top of books that have been "Tiered like bleachers" on the bookshelf. They decide to hold on to the bell and have one of the director's "ring" it whenever the door to the drugstore opens or closes.

### Step 3: Transform the Action into Concrete Reality

The directors are now ready to move on to the third step of the process—enactment of the poem "Oranges." Here, you switch hats from executive designer back to executive director in order to guide the directors through the action process. Remind them that their purpose is not to put on a performance for an audience but to create the action of the poem in a way that will help us see its action and meaning.

I ask the directors to select one person to read the poem and three to enact the roles of the narrator, the girl, and the saleslady. I tell the students who are enacting the characters that they do not need their copies of the text. The directors will coach them through the action, and their job as actors is to pay attention to the directors and use their bodies and voices to enact the story accurately and truthfully.

Next, I ask the directors to place the characters where they need to be before the action begins. They place the girl in the corner of the room where her house is located. She finds the gloves there and holds them in her hands. The narrator, they decide, is coming from home and thus is located on the opposite side of the room, wearing the jacket with the oranges and the nickel stowed in the pockets. The saleslady, they note from the text, is in the back of the drugstore, so they place her along the wall a short way from the counter. We are now ready to begin enacting the poem. I tell the students that as executive director, I will stop the action at times during the enactment to ask them questions about what is happening in the poem and why. I remind them once again that this is not a performance for an audience but a way for us to gain a better understanding of the poem.

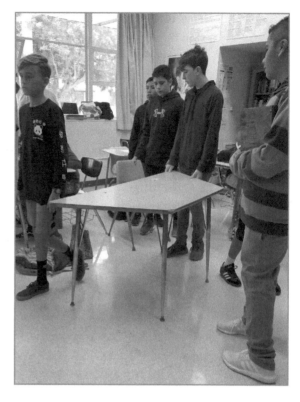

## Enactment

The designated reader begins to read the poem aloud, and the directors, consulting their sequence of the poem's actions, coach the narrator to put the jacket on and walk across the room to the girl's house. The narrator creatively zigzags through the desks to get to her house on the opposite side of the room. The directors then decide they need a dog to bark ("A dog barked at me"), and one of them quickly assumes the part. As the narrator gets close to the girl's house, the directors remind the girl to walk toward the narrator, "pulling / At her gloves," and the two characters are now standing side by side.

### Delving Deeper: Finding More Meaning

I stop the action and ask the directors if there is any dialogue at this point. They check the text and realize there is none. I then ask them how the narrator and the girl communicate without dialogue. They confer and decide that any communication between the narrator and the girl has to be conveyed through physical action. The directors prompt the narrator to smile and touch her shoulder, ("I smiled, / Touched her shoulder"), and I ask them why the narrator does so. They confer again and decide it is to show that the narrator likes the girl. I then ask them if the narrator and the girl walk close to each other or far apart as they go to the drugstore. After further consultation, the directors decide that the pair walk close together to show they like each other without saying anything. The directors then coach the narrator and the girl to walk side by side along the wall toward the drugstore. One of the directors produces a small toy car from his backpack, and another runs outside to find a twig with some leaves, and they place both of these items on the windowsill to represent the "used car lot" and the "line / Of newly planted trees" past which the narrator and the girl walk.

When the narrator and the girl reach the drugstore, the directors instruct the narrator to pantomime opening the door for the girl, and one of the directors rings the bell. I ask why the narrator opens the door for the girl, and they tell me that this is the way it was done back then. They remind the saleslady to walk up behind the counter, but not until she hears the bell ("We / Entered, the tiny bell / Bringing a saleslady / Down a narrow aisle of goods"). The narrator and the girl now stand in front of the counter, and the saleslady stands behind it.

I stop the action again and ask the directors if there is any dialogue at this time. They refer back to the text and notice that the narrator asks "what she wanted." The directors decide the narrator should supply the dialogue, and the reader playing the role asks the girl, "Would you like a candy?" The directors remind the reader playing the girl that this question elicits "Light in her eyes, [and] a smile / Starting at the corners / Of her mouth." I ask the directors what she is thinking, and they think she is very excited that the narrator is going to buy her a candy. At this point, the directors remind the narrator to put hands in pockets and remember that the pocket contains only a nickel ("fingered / A nickel in my pocket"). They prompt the girl to pick up a chocolate candy ("she lifted a chocolate / That cost a dime"), put it on the counter, and move away to look at other things in the store.

Stopping the action again, I ask the directors what the narrator and girl are thinking at this moment. The directors consult with the two readers playing the characters and decide that the narrator is very nervous because the girl has selected a candy that costs too much. The girl, they decide, is oblivious to this dilemma and is having fun looking at other things in the drugstore. They also think that the girl should move away from the counter at this point so that the next action between the narrator and the saleslady can occur without the girl seeing it. The directors then ask the narrator to put the nickel and orange on the counter. They instruct the saleslady to accept this as the payment, and they ask the narrator to give the chocolate to the girl.

I stop the action again to explore what is happening here in more depth. I ask the directors to look at the line "I didn't say anything" and decide whether it marks an important moment in the story. They realize that this is where the narrator, lacking sufficient money to pay for the chocolate, must make a decision. I ask them to propose three choices for the narrator. They decide on the following:

1.  The narrator could ask the girl to put the chocolate back and select a cheaper candy.
2.  The narrator could ask the saleslady to accept the nickel and promise to pay her back later.
3.  The narrator could look for another nickel on the floor.

I then inquire as to how the narrator makes the choice to give the saleslady the nickel and an orange. They speculate as follows:

1.  The narrator looks around at the floor and doesn't see another nickel.
2.  The narrator assumes the saleslady will not accept just one nickel.
3.  The narrator feels too embarrassed to ask the girl to put the chocolate back and select a cheaper candy.

Realizing how much trouble the narrator is in, the directors decide that, while thinking about options, the narrator puts hands in pockets again and remembers that there are two oranges in addition to the nickel. The narrator then wonders if the saleslady might accept the nickel and an orange as payment and decides to give it a try ("I took the nickel from / My pocket, then an orange, / And set them quietly on / The counter"). They tell the narrator to keep looking at the floor while putting the nickel and orange on the counter, then look up at the saleslady. I ask them to consider the line, "When I looked up, / The lady's eyes met mine, / And held them, knowing / Very well what it was all / About." I remind them that there is no dialogue in this moment. Deciding that all of the important communication here is nonverbal, they prompt the narrator to plead with a look for the saleslady to help by accepting the nickel and the orange as payment for the chocolate.

Now I ask the directors if the saleslady also has a decision to make. They point out that she understands the offering, as indicated in the text: "knowing / Very well what it was all / About." I ask what the saleslady is thinking. The directors confer with the student portraying her and propose the following:

1. The saleslady could tell the narrator that another nickel is needed in order to buy the candy.
2. The saleslady could accept the nickel and the orange as payment.

I ask them to justify the decision she makes. They confer a bit more and decide on the following:

1. The saleslady knows the narrator's mother and knows that the narrator is a good person.
2. The saleslady doesn't want to embarrass the narrator in front of the girl.
3. The saleslady can easily add five cents to the cash register.

With this understanding of the dynamics of the moment, the directors tell the saleslady and the narrator to hold the look between them. Then, when the saleslady makes her decision, she should nod to the narrator. The narrator can then breathe a sigh of relief, pick up the chocolate, and give it to the girl.

We now repeat the action sequence from the time the girl selects the chocolate. The action this time is very different. It is slower and more deliberate, and we can see what is happening as each character thinks through choices and makes a decision. We see the narrator look at the floor in a desperate search for another nickel and then plead with the saleslady with a look while placing the one nickel and the orange on the counter. We see the saleslady look kindly at the narrator and make her decision to accept the payment. I ask them why this second rendering of the action was better, and they agree that they could now see the decision making behind the actions and why this silent interaction constitutes an important turning point in the poem. They agree that although there is no dialogue here, the long pause and the subtle action during that pause create an opportunity for the narrator and the saleslady to communicate. Thus we can clearly see how the writer, at this crucial point in the poem, tells the story through action and not dialogue.

The directors now prompt the narrator and the girl to leave the drugstore, and they remind the bell ringer to ring the bell as they open the door to exit. Next, they tell the narrator and the girl to walk back toward her house, holding hands ("I took my girl's hand / In mine for two blocks"). The hand-holding causes some tension, but we get past it. When the characters reach the halfway point between the drugstore and the girl's house, the directors tell them to stop, then ask the girl to unwrap the chocolate and eat it while the narrator peels the orange. Although the text of the poem does not say they stop, the directors decide that if they stop walking when the girl unwraps the chocolate and the narrator peels the orange, it will give the last actions of the story a stronger focus.

When we finish, we go back and consult our sequence of actions to ensure that we have included everything. We note that indeed we have, and we congratulate ourselves. As we do so, several of the directors remark that what had been a mere list of action phrases yesterday has come to life today, and as a result they can see what is happening between the characters much more clearly. I make sure that we leave enough time at the end of class to restore the room to its original arrangement. I give the students a homework assignment to write one page: "Now that you are more aware of the importance of action in a story, how can you apply this to other literature you read?"

## Students Generate Action with "Thank You, M'am"

### Day One

I inform this group of students that we are going to wade into new territory today and tomorrow by doing something very different with reading. I have their attention. I tell them we are going to borrow some reading ideas from the world of the theater, and I describe how theater artists must read in a very specific way to be able to transform literary works into stage productions. I explain that we are going to focus on what a stage director does and that directors have very specific goals when they read because they must find and generate the action of a story. I define both physical and verbal action and tell them that directors must not only find the action in a text but also determine how it will be represented on the stage.

I give each student a copy of "Thank You, M'am," and we read it aloud together "as ourselves." I then provide some background information about the story and its writer, Langston Hughes. Next, I tell them we will read the story again but this time engage in a little role-playing and read it as directors. I tell them that I will assume the role of executive director to answer questions and guide them in their reading tasks. I explain that when we read the story this time, we will no longer read as "students and teacher in a classroom"; instead, we all will now read as directors in pursuit of specific reading goals:

1. Search for and record evidence of physical and verbal action from the text.

2. Conceptualize the physical and verbal action.

3. Transform the action into concrete reality.

I give students the director's worklist (the same one used for "Oranges") specifying the details of their reading tasks as directors. (If you customize the worklist for a certain piece of literature, be sure to include the appropriate designer's questions in the director's worklist and confirm the directors' understanding that as they search for evidence of action they also need to envision a space in which it can occur.) The students are somewhat apprehensive about these unusual instructions but agree to give it a try. We now begin our process of reading as directors.

## Step 1: Search for and Record Evidence of Physical and Verbal Action from the Text

I divide this class into groups of three and give them fifteen minutes to achieve the first of the director's tasks—identifying a sequence of actions in the story. I give them the option of writing directly on the text, taking notes on their tablets or with pen and paper, or using a worksheet (for an example, see Figure 7.3). I remind them that as they create their list of actions, they also need to be thinking about an environment in which the action can occur.

### WHAT THEY FIND

The sequence of actions that each group finds is essentially the same. Here is a listing of the actions identified, using phrasing from the text itself and underlining the verbs.

1. *What is the sequence of actions that takes the characters from the beginning of the text to the end. (Look specifically for action verbs and <u>underline</u> them.)*

    a. "a boy <u>ran</u> up behind her and <u>tried to snatch</u> her purse"

    b. "the boy <u>fell</u> on his back on the sidewalk"

    c. "his legs <u>flew up</u>"

    d. "The large woman simply <u>turned around and kicked</u> him right square in his blue-jeaned sitter"

    e. "she <u>reached down, picked the boy up</u> by his shirtfront"

    f. "<u>shook</u> him until his teeth rattled"

    g. "she <u>bent</u> down enough to permit him <u>to stoop</u> and <u>pick up</u> her purse"

Published 1958 pre-story Roger - looking for shine. Mrs J - closing shop

## Thank You, Ma'am (by Langston Hughes)

She was a large woman with a large purse that had everything in it but hammer and nails. It had a long strap, and she carried it slung across her shoulder. It was about eleven o'clock at night, and she was walking alone, when a boy ran up behind her and tried to snatch her purse. The strap broke with the single tug the boy gave it from behind. But the boy's weight and the weight of the purse combined caused him to lose his balance so, intseqd of taking off full blast as he had hoped, the boy fell on his back on the sidewalk, and his legs flew up. the large woman simply turned around and kicked him right square in his blue-jeaned sitter. Then she reached down, picked the boy up by his shirt front, and shook him until his teeth rattled.

J - walking
R - attacks
R - falls
J - kicks him
J - picks him up by shirt front
J - bend down
R - picks up bag

After that the woman said, "Pick up my pocketbook, boy, and give it here." She still held him. But she bent down enough to permit him to stoop and pick up her purse. Then she said, "Now ain't you ashamed of yourself?"

Firmly gripped by his shirt front, the boy said, "Yes'm."

The woman said, "What did you want to do it for?"

The boy said, "I didn't aim to."

She said, "You a lie!"

By that time two or three people passed, stopped, turned to look, and some stood watching.

"If I turn you loose, will you run?" asked the woman.

"Yes'm," said the boy.

"Then I won't turn you loose," said the woman. She did not release him.

"I'm very sorry, lady, I'm sorry," whispered the boy.

"Um-hum! And your face is dirty. I got a great mind to wash your face for you. Ain't you got nobody home to tell you to wash your face?"

"No'm," said the boy.

"Then it will get washed this evening," said the large woman starting up the street, dragging the frightened boy behind her.

J - starts walking w/ him

He looked as if he were fourteen or fifteen, frail and willow-wild, in tennis shoes and blue jeans.

The woman said, "You ought to be my son. I would teach you right from wrong. Least I can do right now is to wash your face. Are you hungry?"

"No'm," said the being dragged boy. "I just want you to turn me loose."

"Was I bothering *you* when I turned that corner?" asked the woman.

"No'm."

A

**FIGURE 7.3.** Notes about character written directly on the text.

**FIGURE 7.3.** Continued.

"But you put yourself in contact with *me*," said the woman. "If you think that that contact is not going to last awhile, you got another thought coming. When I get through with you, sir, you are going to remember Mrs. Luella Bates Washington Jones."

Sweat popped out on the boy's face and he began to struggle. Mrs. Jones stopped, jerked him around in front of her, put a half-nelson about his neck, and continued to drag him up the street. When she got to her door, she dragged the boy inside, down a hall, and into a large kitchenette-furnished room at the rear of the house. She switched on the light and left the door open. The boy could hear other roomers laughing and talking in the large house. Some of their doors were open, too, so he knew he and the woman were not alone. The woman still had him by the neck in the middle of her room.

She said, "What is your name?"

"Roger," answered the boy.

"Then, Roger, you go to that sink and wash your face," said the woman, whereupon she turned him loose—at last. Roger looked at the door—looked at the woman—looked at the door—*and went to the sink.*

Let the water run until it gets warm," she said. "Here's a clean towel."

"You gonna take me to jail?" asked the boy, bending over the sink.

"Not with that face, I would not take you nowhere," said the woman. "Here I am trying to get home to cook me a bite to eat and you snatch my pocketbook! Maybe, you ain't been to your supper either, late as it be. Have you?"

"There's nobody home at my house," said the boy.

"Then we'll eat," said the woman, "I believe you're hungry—or been hungry—to try to snatch my pockekbook."

"I wanted a pair of blue suede shoes," said the boy.

"Well, you didn't have to snatch *my* pocketbook to get some suede shoes," said Mrs. Luella Bates Washington Jones. "You could of asked me."

"M'am?"

The water dripping from his face, the boy looked at her. There was a long pause. A very long pause. After he had dried his face and not knowing what else to do dried it again, the boy turned around, wondering what next. The door was open. He could make a dash for it down the hall. He could run, run, run, run, *run!*

The woman was sitting on the day-bed. After a while she said, "I were young once and I wanted things I could not get."

There was another long pause. The boy's mouth opened. Then he frowned, but not knowing he frowned.

The woman said, "Um-hum! You thought I was going to say *but*, didn't you? You thought I was

B

*Handwritten margin notes:*
- dragging him up street. Get to her house. Brings him in
- Lets go of him. Roger. To sink
- J. give him towel
- J. sit on daybed
- pause

**FIGURE 7.3.** Continued.

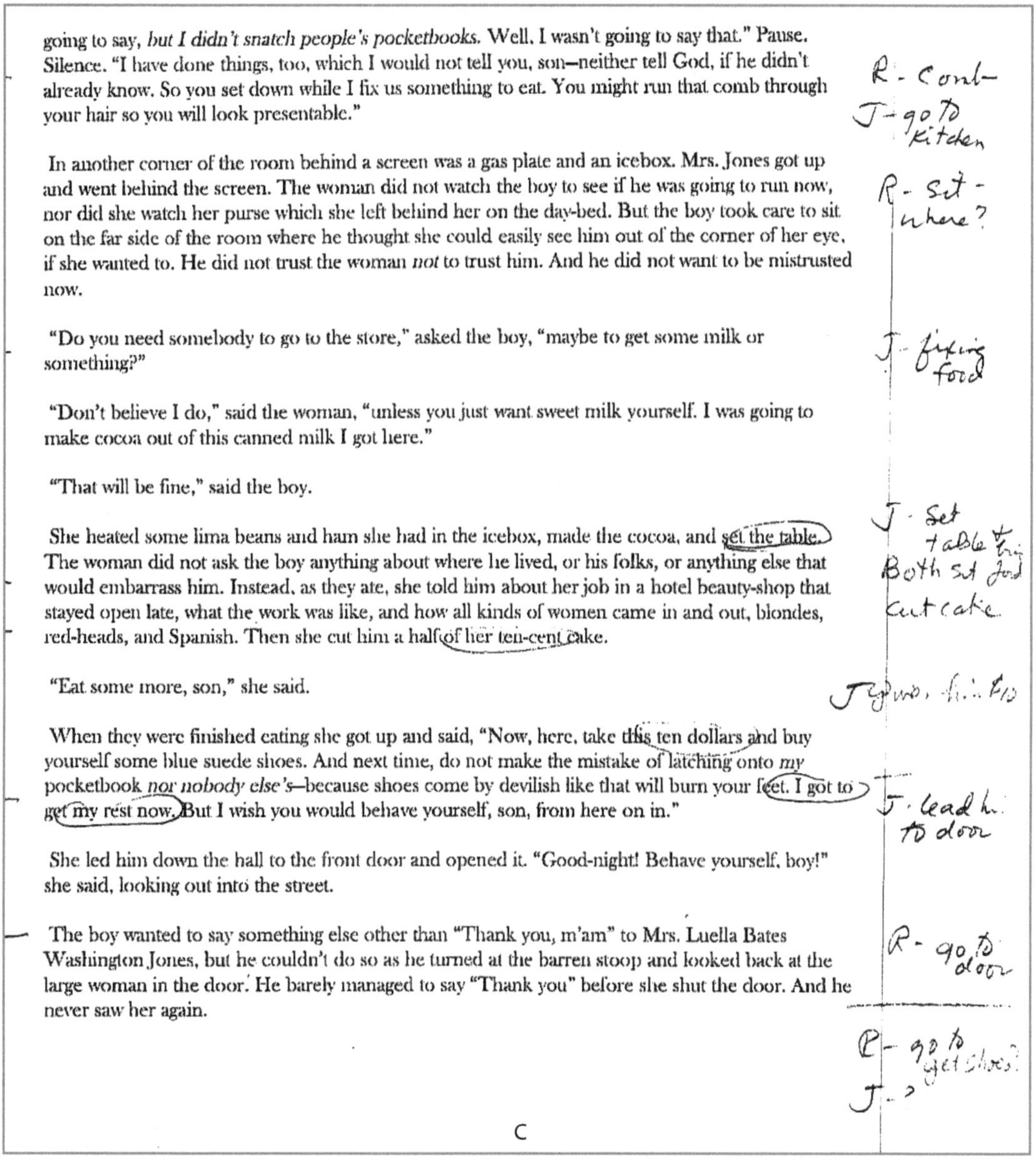

going to say, *but I didn't snatch people's pocketbooks. Well, I wasn't going to say that.*" Pause. Silence. "I have done things, too, which I would not tell you, son—neither tell God, if he didn't already know. So you set down while I fix us something to eat. You might run that comb through your hair so you will look presentable."

In another corner of the room behind a screen was a gas plate and an icebox. Mrs. Jones got up and went behind the screen. The woman did not watch the boy to see if he was going to run now, nor did she watch her purse which she left behind her on the day-bed. But the boy took care to sit on the far side of the room where he thought she could easily see him out of the corner of her eye, if she wanted to. He did not trust the woman *not* to trust him. And he did not want to be mistrusted now.

"Do you need somebody to go to the store," asked the boy, "maybe to get some milk or something?"

"Don't believe I do," said the woman, "unless you just want sweet milk yourself. I was going to make cocoa out of this canned milk I got here."

"That will be fine," said the boy.

She heated some lima beans and ham she had in the icebox, made the cocoa, and set the table. The woman did not ask the boy anything about where he lived, or his folks, or anything else that would embarrass him. Instead, as they ate, she told him about her job in a hotel beauty-shop that stayed open late, what the work was like, and how all kinds of women came in and out, blondes, red-heads, and Spanish. Then she cut him a half of her ten-cent cake.

"Eat some more, son," she said.

When they were finished eating she got up and said, "Now, here, take this ten dollars and buy yourself some blue suede shoes. And next time, do not make the mistake of latching onto *my* pocketbook *nor nobody else's*—because shoes come by devilish like that will burn your feet. I got to get my rest now. But I wish you would behave yourself, son, from here on in."

She led him down the hall to the front door and opened it. "Good-night! Behave yourself, boy!" she said, looking out into the street.

The boy wanted to say something else other than "Thank you, m'am" to Mrs. Luella Bates Washington Jones, but he couldn't do so as he turned at the barren stoop and looked back at the large woman in the door. He barely managed to say "Thank you" before she shut the door. And he never saw her again.

C

*Handwritten margin notes:*
R - Cont-
J - go to Kitchen
R - Sit - where?
J - fixing food
J - Set table too
Both sit too
cut cake
J - gives, h... too
J - lead h... to door
R - go to door
R - go to get shoes?
J - ?

---

h. "<u>starting</u> up the street, <u>dragging</u> the frightened boy behind her"

i. "<u>put</u> a half nelson about his neck"

j. "continued to <u>drag</u> him up the street"

k. "<u>dragged</u> the boy inside, down a hall, and into a large kitchenette-furnished room at the rear of the house"

l. "She <u>switched</u> on the light"

m. "she <u>turned</u> him loose"

n. "'Roger, you <u>go</u> to that sink and <u>wash</u> your face,' <u>said</u> the woman"

o. "Roger <u>looked</u> at the door—<u>looked</u> at the woman—<u>looked</u> at the door—*and <u>went</u> to the sink.*"

p. "he <u>dried</u> his face . . . <u>dried</u> it again . . . <u>turned</u> around"

q. "Mrs. Jones <u>got up</u> and <u>went</u> behind the screen"

r. "the boy <u>took care</u> to <u>sit</u> on the far side of the room"

s. "She <u>heated</u> some lima beans and ham she had in the icebox, <u>made</u> the cocoa"

t. "<u>set</u> the table"

u. "they <u>ate</u>"

v. "'Now here, <u>take</u> this ten dollars'"

w. "She <u>led</u> him down the hall to the front door and <u>opened</u> it"

x. "he <u>went</u> down the steps"

y. "she <u>shut</u> the door"

2. *Revisit your list of actions, this time from the last action to the first. Has each action been motivated by the previous one, thus verifying the continuity of the text?*

Next, I ask the groups to start with their last action and verify that each action was motivated by the one before. Through this process, they make a major discovery. Look at actions designated *p* through *r* in the list. Initially, students list *p* ("dried his face") immediately followed by *q* ("Mrs. Jones got up and went behind the screen"). On closer review, however, they recognize that the list includes no motivation for Mrs. Jones to get up and go behind the screen. Referring back to the text, they discover the motivating action between the other two actions: "'So you set down while I fix us something to eat.'" This example demonstrates how the process of starting at the end and working back to the beginning verifies that each action has been motivated by a previous one. Thus it is an important discovery step for directors, as well as a part of the continual discovery of new details and nuances in the text as they work through the process.

Keeping an eye on the clock to confirm that we have enough time to accomplish today's tasks, I address the next two questions with the whole class rather than putting them back into groups.

3. *What does each character's voice sound like?*

   Students agree that Mrs. Jones's voice is louder than Roger's to indicate her control of the situation. Yet as she gets to know him and feel more comfortable in his presence, her voice gets softer. Roger's voice, they think, is quiet, tentative, and generally passive.

4. *What is happening during any pauses?*

   The writer clearly indicates several pauses: "There was a long pause. A very long pause. . . . There was another long pause. . . . Pause. Silence." We decide that in each case, characters are making decisions during the pauses and determining how they will respond to a specific situation. I ask students to remember this when we generate the action itself so that this "thinking time" becomes part of the action to help us see what is going on in the characters' minds.

## Step 2: Conceptualize the Physical and Verbal Action

As we get to this second stage of the director's reading process, I put on my executive designer hat and help the directors conceptualize an environment for the action. They have been thinking about this as they generate their sequence of actions, and now we will hear their ideas. I take them through a mini version of the designer's process, focusing them toward envisioning an environment for "Thank You, M'am" in the classroom. I conduct this part of the process as a whole-class discussion but ask them to consult in their groups of three before they answer questions.

I ask the directors how many locations we need in order to create the environment. They consult the text and each other and decide that we need two locations: a street corner where Mrs. Jones and Roger initially meet and her room in the boardinghouse. They also determine that we need a substantial pathway between the two locations because various kinds of action and dialogue occur during the walk. I ask them how they think we can reconfigure our classroom to create these spaces. They confer again, consulting their notes and each other, then suggest placing the street area in one corner of the room and Mrs. Jones's room in another corner. However, as they think about it further and look at all of the action that occurs as the characters make the walk between the two spaces, they don't think that configuration will allow enough space for the action in the street and the dialogue that has to occur as Mrs. Jones drags Roger to her house. In addition, as they reread the text and remember how much furniture is contained in Mrs. Jones's room, they realize that a corner will probably not give them enough space to accommodate everything.

I let the students toss some ideas around, then intercede as executive designer. Reminding them that this is not a performance for an audience but a way to help us see and understand the story's action and meaning, I suggest that we think a little more outside the box. I float the idea of moving the desks to create an open space in the middle of the room and also create a pathway around the room's perimeter. This way we can use the open space for their initial meeting on the street; then, while Mrs. Jones is dragging Roger around the perimeter of the room, we can set up the boardinghouse room in the center space and the characters can walk into it. I remind the students again that there is no audience, so we can use the space in whatever way works best. You can coach the readers with ideas or try to let them be the ones to figure out how to create the environment in the classroom. Some students need more help with this process than others do, so use your judgment to decide when it is appropriate for you to intervene with ideas to help them.

I then ask students to think about what needs to be in Mrs. Jones's room and to decide whether they think it will all fit in a space in the center of the classroom. Consulting the text again, they make a list of what the room needs: a daybed, a sink, a table, two chairs, and a small kitchenette area with places for a gas plate, an icebox, pots, a pitcher, cups, plates, silverware, napkins, ham, lima beans, cocoa, and cake. Since there's no audience, I remind students that we can stop the action when we get to that point in the story, set up the boardinghouse room, and see if everything will fit. They agree to try the idea, and I ask each group to create a rough sketch of how they would create Mrs. Jones's boardinghouse room in the center of the classroom. I tell them to be sure to bring these sketches tomorrow.

## Day Two

### Constructing the Context

When students come into the classroom, they immediately gather in their groups of three and look over their sketches. Today's tasks, I remind them, are to decide on and create an environment for "Thank You, M'am" and then generate the story's action within that environment. I remind them to look around and notice that there is no audience. Our goal is not to stage a performance for an audience but to give ourselves a way to see the story and better understand its meaning.

We then begin to reconfigure the classroom, moving desks so that we have an open space in the middle of the room and a walking path around the room's perimeter (see Figure 7.4). As we create this space, we decide that it may be more efficient to create the walkway along only three walls and give ourselves one

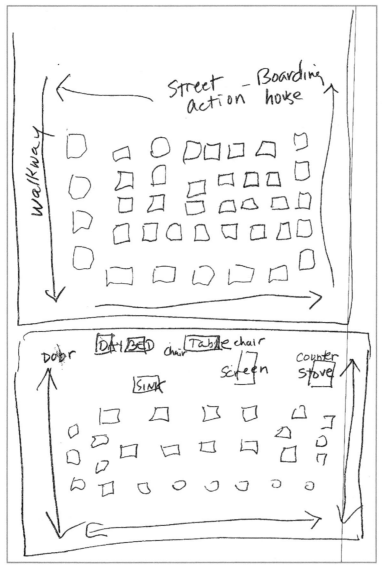

**FIGURE 7.4.** Diagram of classroom configuration allowing for needed spaces and actions.

wall as part of the boardinghouse room. We create an open area stretching from one of the walls into the center of the room and clear a pathway around the other three walls. I suggest that we begin the enactment of the story in the open center space and see if we have enough space for the walk that Mrs. Jones and Roger make if we give them only the three walls for this action. If that works, we can continue the action in the boardinghouse when we get to that point in the story.

It is okay to create a story in pieces like this and set up spaces in the classroom as the story unfolds. Sometimes, in fact, it may be the only way you can accommodate all of the locations of a story in the classroom. Always remember that you are not performing for an audience but creating an experiential way for readers to see and understand the action.

Next, I show the directors the bag of props I have brought in and tell them that the only prop they can have at this point is Mrs. Jones's large purse. I will hold the rest of the props in the bag until we get to the action in the boardinghouse. This, of course, makes them that much more interested in what props I have stashed in the bag for the rest of the story!

## Step 3: Transform the Action into Concrete Reality

### ENACTMENT

Although we don't have the entire environment set up in the classroom, we have enough to begin the action, and I ask the directors to select one person to read the story aloud as we enact it as well as two readers to serve as actors who will portray the characters. They do so, and I now switch hats to become the executive director again in order to help the directors coach the characters through the action. I remind the readers portraying the characters not to bring their copies of the text, so that they can concentrate on physically and vocally creating the action indicated by the directors. I also tell the students that I will be stopping the action at times so we can explore what is happening in the story in more depth.

I ask the directors to place the two characters in their proper locations before the story begins. They think that Mrs. Jones is walking home from her job at the beauty shop ("she told him about her job in a hotel beauty shop that stayed open late") and that Roger is hanging out on the street, sees her with the big purse, and pegs her as a good prospect for a purse snatching. The directors give Mrs. Jones the large purse and place her in a corner of the room; they place Roger among the desks where he can see her walk into the center of the room. Before we start, I show the students that the purse has a strap attached by clasps, so that if Mrs. Jones unhooks one of the clasps and holds the strap to the purse when she walks, the strap can appear to break when Roger pulls at it.

The designated reader begins the story. The directors refer to their list of sequential actions, tell Mrs. Jones to walk into the center area, and then instruct the two characters to follow the descriptive directions as they are read: "A boy ran up behind her and tried to snatch her purse. The strap broke with the sudden single tug the boy gave it from behind. But the boy's weight and the weight of the purse combined caused him to lose his balance. . . . [T]he boy fell on his back on the sidewalk and his legs flew up. The large woman simply turned around and kicked him right square in his blue-jeaned sitter. Then she reached down, picked the boy up by his shirtfront, and shook him until his teeth rattled."

Accordingly, the student portraying Roger runs up behind the student playing Mrs. Jones and grabs the purse, which "breaks." He falls onto his back, and his legs fly up. Mrs. Jones kicks him in the seat, reaches down and picks him up by the shirtfront, and shakes him. We enact this action as truthfully as we can while exercising due restraint. No one should ever get hurt in these enactments, so our Mrs. Jones doesn't quite shake him hard enough to make his teeth rattle! Even so, the student playing the role of Roger says that the actual shaking is really scary and makes Mrs. Jones a fearsome opponent. Moreover, the actor notes that this level of fear had not been evident in the reading of the text.

The directors continue to guide the actors through the physical action and dialogue provided by the text as Mrs. Jones forces Roger to pick up the purse, admonishes him for what he has done, establishes that he will run away if she lets him loose, and ultimately decides to take him back to her house. The directors also notice here that the text says some people stop and watch the action ("By that time two or three people passed, stopped, turned to look, and some stood watching"). As a result, several of the directors place themselves near the characters and watch the action as bystanders. The student playing Roger now says that he is even more scared of Mrs. Jones with people watching them and admits that he is in no way inclined to argue with her.

### DELVING DEEPER: FINDING MORE MEANING

I stop the action here and ask the directors to remember what they wrote yesterday about the vocal qualities of the two characters. They decide that Mrs. Jones should speak louder and with more force than Roger, whose voice reflects how scared he is after she prevents his attempt to steal her purse. While the action is stopped, I also ask the directors why Mrs. Jones decides to take Roger to her house rather than to the police station. After all, he has just tried to steal her purse. They confer and decide that she feels sorry for him. I tell them to remember this moment and note that we will revisit why she takes him home after we have enacted more of the story.

The directors continue generating the physical and verbal action with the actors and prompt Mrs. Jones to drag Roger around the perimeter of the room by his shirtfront. They ask me how to perform a half nelson, and I show them how to do it safely. (I looked it up on the web the night before because I knew they'd ask me! You can also ask students to research any actions that are unfamiliar to them.) Mrs. Jones puts a half nelson around Roger's neck at the appropriate time and yanks him the rest of the way home, further terrifying our actor playing Roger.

At this point, we congratulate ourselves, because we realize that the walkway we have created around the room's three sides allows the characters enough space and time to accomplish the needed action and dialogue. I stop the action again and ask the directors if the sequence of actions we are enacting follows what they have discovered in the text. Referring back to their list of actions, they verify that so far it does.

We are now ready to continue the story, so we give the two actors a break while we figure out how to set up the boardinghouse in the space we have designated for it. I ask the directors to refer back to their sketches and to the text so that we can decide how to set up the space to represent Mrs. Jones's room and accommodate all of the furniture and required action. On the board, we re-create the list we made earlier of what the room needs.

Now it's time to construct the boardinghouse environment. Students place two single chairs against the wall to represent the daybed, set a desk next to the daybed to represent the table, and put a chair on either side of the table. They take books off of a short bookshelf and move it to create the screen that separates the kitchenette area from the rest of the room. They find a small table to represent the kitchen counter with the icebox and the gas plate. I then give them the much-anticipated remaining props: a pitcher, pots, plates, cups, napkins, silverware, a towel, a bag of cookies and a chocolate bar for the food, a washcloth, a comb, a bowl, and a serving spoon. They place all of the kitchen items on the table in the kitchenette area, and one of the directors runs out to the hall to fill the pitcher from the water fountain to represent the cocoa. They look at the towel, washcloth, and comb, refer back to the text, and realize they have forgotten the sink! Looking around the room, they find a trash can, place a large atlas on top of it to form a surface for the sink, place a bowl on it, and set it in front of the daybed. They place the washcloth and comb on the sink and put the towel near the door.

After everything is set up in the boardinghouse room, we continue the action with the actors. The reader resumes the story, providing the actors with dialogue from the text. As the characters come close to the boardinghouse, some of the directors decide that they will take on the roles of boarders in the other rooms, and they begin to laugh and talk ("The boy could hear other roomers laughing and talking in the large house"). Once Mrs. Jones leads Roger (still in the half nelson) into her room, the noise and the boarders vanish. When the characters enter the boardinghouse room, the directors coach Mrs. Jones to release Roger from the half nelson and tell him to go to the sink.

I stop the action again and ask the directors to remember yesterday's conversation about the importance of the pauses in the story and how they help define significant moments when characters make decisions. I ask them what is happening here as Roger looks "at the door . . . at the woman . . . at the door" and then goes "to the sink." I ask them why they think Roger doesn't run away when he has the chance. Some think he wants to show Mrs. Jones that he can be good. The actor playing Roger admits that he is still terrified and does not want to anger her again.

I ask them to think about options for positioning the two characters in a way that shows, through the physical action, what is going on in Roger's head as he makes his decision. We debate whether or not to locate Mrs. Jones between Roger and the door when he realizes that he could possibly run out. The directors agree to position the characters so that there is an open space between Roger and the door, thus showing that he stays due to a decision on his part, not because Mrs. Jones has physically blocked the doorway. To create this space, the directors prompt Mrs. Jones to walk over to the daybed and put down her purse, which, according to the story text, she leaves "behind her on the daybed"—a new discovery for the directors and another example of the ongoing discovery process.

We start the action again from the line in the story that says, "'Then, Roger, you go to that sink and wash your face.'" Roger completes the action of looking at the door, looking at Mrs. Jones, and looking at the door again, then decides to go to the sink. Through these actions, we now see him make the decision. One of the directors also points out the importance of our decision to place the towel near the door. With the towel in that location, when Roger finishes washing his face, he needs to go toward the door to retrieve the towel. This gives him another opportunity to run, and to make an additional decision to stay, once again revealing meaning through the story's action.

I also stop the action at other places where the writer of the text has indicated a pause, "long pause," or "very long pause" and remind the directors to consider whether these are important moments of decision in the story. More specifically, I ask them to define what is happening during each of the pauses and to consider how they can use physical action to express what the characters are thinking and deciding during the silence. We discuss how silence can be a powerful way to express verbal action if we acknowledge the characters' thinking process during these pauses.

When we get to the action of Mrs. Jones moving into the kitchenette area to fix something to eat, the directors compare options for where exactly Roger should "sit on the far side of the room, away from the purse, where he thought she could easily see him out of the corner of her eye if she wanted to." They find a spot at the table where Mrs. Jones can see him from the kitchen area. The directors remind Mrs. Jones that she has a lot to accomplish when she is in the kitchenette: cook the ham and lima beans, set the table, serve the ham and lima beans, pour the cocoa, and cut and serve the ten-cent cake. The student playing Roger comments that seeing her take all of these actions makes him realize how kind she is being and how much she is doing for him.

As the characters eat, the directors prompt Mrs. Jones to improvise the dialogue telling Roger about the beauty shop where she works ("she told him about her job in a hotel beauty shop"). The actor playing Mrs. Jones creates a wonderful, detailed account of the ladies who come into the beauty shop. As Roger and Mrs. Jones eat, I stop the action again and ask the actors what each character is thinking. The student playing Mrs. Jones admits that she appreciates having some company. She also feels good about providing Roger with a decent meal, which he probably doesn't often get. Roger admits to still being scared of Mrs. Jones yet is very appreciative of the kindness she has shown him. We discuss how much happens in the story that is not spoken but can be expressed through physical action. During this discussion, you can direct questions either to the students creating the characters or to the directors.

When the characters finish eating, the directors prompt Mrs. Jones to stand up and retrieve the ten dollars from her purse, which she has left on the daybed. Mrs. Jones brings the money back to the table, gives it to Roger, and tells him, "Now here, take this ten dollars and buy yourself some blue suede shoes. And next time, do not make the mistake of latching onto *my* pocketbook *nor nobody else's*—because shoes got by devilish ways will burn your feet." We discuss what she is thinking while she says this and what Roger is thinking while he listens.

I ask the students to reconsider the question we left unanswered yesterday: Why does Mrs. Jones take Roger home and feed him rather than taking him to the police station? One director refers back to Mrs. Jones's comment, "I have done things, too, which I would not tell you, son—neither tell God, if He didn't already know. Everybody's got something in common." This student speculates that perhaps Mrs. Jones had a similar experience when she was younger, and perhaps someone was not kind to her.

The directors then guide the actors through the action described at the end of the story, prompting Mrs. Jones to lead Roger to the door and open it and asking Roger to walk away from the door and then turn to look back at Mrs. Jones. I ask Roger why he turned back as if to say something but instead stayed silent. He says that he was still frightened by Mrs. Jones, yet very affected by how kindly she treated him, and that he wanted to tell her so. He also says that he wanted to say, "Thank you, ma'am," to show his respect for her but she didn't give him time, instead closing the door before he could say it. A caveat here: Alternative versions of this story exist, including at least one in which, unlike the official version we are using, Roger manages to say "thank you" before Mrs. Jones closes the door. Be sure that your depicted action reflects the specific text you are using.

Once we have finished the enactment and restored the classroom to its original order, I ask the students what they have learned from generating the action of the story. The student playing Roger says that when he read the words on the page, he couldn't understand why Roger didn't run away when he had the chance, but experiencing the physical action of the shaking, the dragging, and the half nelson made him realize how much Mrs. Jones intimidated him. Another student says that all the pauses didn't register in print but that filling in what was happening during those pauses—specifically, allowing time for the characters to think and make decisions—gave the pauses significance. Several students comment that stopping the action to delve into what was happening helped them identify important moments in the story.

This class now receives a homework assignment asking them to write one page articulating what they have learned from putting "Thank You M'am" into action that they hadn't realized when they initially read the text.

## Generating Action with Novels

Enacting an entire novel in the classroom, although possible, presents a significant challenge. The director's process, however, can help illuminate parts of novels that students find especially difficult to understand. Asking students to plot out the specific sequence of physical and verbal actions that make up a challenging section of a novel can often help them follow and understand its continuity. In addition, selecting short scenes from a novel and enacting them in different ways provides excellent opportunities to explore meaning and how it can be represented through physical and verbal action. To that end, any of the strategies used here for "Oranges" and "Thank You, M'am" can be applied to novels. Here are some additional ways to use the director's process to help focus reading on the discovery of action in novels:

1. Ask small groups to enact sequential scenes from a novel. Explore how the action of a previous scene motivates the subsequent scene.

2. Ask small groups to enact the same scene and justify the actions involved. What textual evidence informs each action? Compare results. Which action choices best reveal the author's intent and the story's meaning?

3. Ask small groups or individuals to write an account of the action of the same scene or of sequential scenes. Then ask each group or individual to verify the causality of the actions by starting at the end and checking whether each action is motivated by the previous one. Compare results.

4. Either in writing or through enactment, ask students to create action that could have happened before the novel begins. Do this activity in groups and compare ideas. What textual information is used to decide?

5. Either in writing or through enactment, create action that might happen after the novel ends. Do this activity in groups and compare ideas. How is information from the text used to decide what happens?

## Generating Action in an Online Environment

While the director's process may pose challenges in an online environment, its value to reading comprehension is well worth the effort. Tangible action can still be created for a story when you don't have a physical classroom, but in a different way.

You can orient students to the use of drama and to the director's reading process in a synchronous session with the whole class. Be sure to define both physical and verbal action and include the necessary parts of the designer's process so that students are envisioning an environment as they think through the story's actions. They can then search for evidence of the story's action in the text either individually or by using use your computer platform to work in small groups. Afterward, they can share their ideas and decide on a single sequence of actions that carries the story from its beginning to its end, making sure to revisit the actions in reverse order from last to first in order to verify causality. Remind each group that as they search for and find the story's actions, they must also envision an environment in which the action can occur.

Once they have identified the story's actions, they can create them virtually. In the theater, directors, choreographers, and stage managers use any of numerous apps to track a production's movement patterns, but once again, these software programs are costly, complex, and unnecessary for our reading process. However, as discussed in regard to the designer's process, students can create their ideas for an environment in any of a number of simple apps that allow users to populate a space with furniture and people. Alternatively, they can create a simple sketch of the environment and draw arrows to identify the action patterns of the characters. They can also write out a description of the action. With any of these approaches, you can ask students to create their action patterns asynchronously and then bring them together in a synchronous class session to share their ideas.

While engaging with the director's process remotely does not give you the live interaction component of enactment in the classroom—and will probably yield more discussion than physical action—it will still give students the experience of reading interactively as directors, identifying a story's sequence of actions, and visualizing those actions in an environment.

## Wrap-Up

The director's process of finding and creating a story's action challenges students not only to find the actions in a story but also to look beyond and between the words to generate a tangible representation that expresses the story's meaning through the actions. When students engage in the director's process, they must also examine the text from the designer's perspective in order to visualize an environment to accommodate the action. As students experiment with different choices and compare options to determine the best representation of the story's action, they build skills that help them identify a story's structure and meaning as well.

The director's process is one of continual discovery. In students' initial reading, it is doubtful that they will uncover all of the story's actions. As a result, as they work through the process and generate the physical and verbal actions with actors in a physical environment, they will continue to find nuances and make new discoveries within the text.

# 8

# Application of the Collaborative Process

*Building Characters' Lives, Constructing Context, and Generating Action Together*

The collaborative process is the most complex, yet the most comprehensive, way to implement the reading strategies. As a result, it provides students and teachers with the greatest challenge and the most reward. When students engage in the collaborative process, they are not only given the authority of a specific theater artist but take on shared responsibility as well, realizing that if their obligations are not met, others are adversely affected. In this collaborative process, students have the most agency and the most accountability, as they must solve problems, make decisions both individually and collectively, and work together to achieve the final result. As you read through this section, you will see how responsibility for the outcome shifts from the teacher to the students.

## Students Collaborate on "Oranges"

### Day One

I start this class session by telling students we are going to do something very different with a piece of literature today and tomorrow. I explain that we are going to read a poem, "Oranges" by Gary Soto, once "as ourselves" and then again in a very different way. I seem to have their attention, and we read the poem aloud together as ourselves. I give them some background on the poem and the writer.

Next, I explain that we are going to borrow some reading strategies from the world of the theater, and I describe how theater artists use specific reading techniques so they can build characters' lives, envision and construct a story's context, and generate its action for the stage.

I tell students that when we read the poem again, we will no longer be reading as ourselves but will engage in role-playing as theater artists who read to accomplish certain tasks and achieve specific goals. Some of them, reading as actors, will search the text for character evidence, create character biographies and relationships, and fill in any time gaps in the story. Others, reading as designers, will search the text for evidence of context, envision what the context will look like, and construct it in our classroom. Still others, reading as directors, will search the text for evidence of action, generate a sequence of the poem's actions, and create its enactment in the classroom. I will serve as producer to help them coordinate their goals and actions with each other and guide them toward the ultimate objective of creating the poem's characters in action in their environment.

They question my sanity but agree to go along.

## Step 1. Divide the Class into Three Groups and Assign Each Group a Worklist

Dividing the class into three groups, I designate who will be actors, who will be designers, and who will be directors. I tell the students that each group will get a worklist detailing the specific tasks they need to accomplish as these artists. I explain further that we will use today for preparation work, and tomorrow we will combine our work to generate an enactment of the poem in an environment we create in the classroom. I give each group their appropriate worklist; the worklists are the same ones I use for each individual reading process and can be found near the beginning of Chapters 5, 6, and 7, respectively, as well as in the appendix. I tell students that each worklist begins with instructions to search for and find certain evidence in the text and designates specific details to look for and questions to answer as they read the text for evidence of character, context, or action. Reminding them that they need to take notes as they find what they are looking for in the text, I specify that they may write directly onto the text, take notes separately, or use worksheets.

I also tell the students that I will come around to each group individually to further explain their specific process and answer any questions, and that as I do so, they should all start reading and searching the text for the evidence they need to find.

We begin our reading as collaborative partners.

### FIRST CONSULTATION WITH THE ACTORS

I confer first with the designated group of actors, review their worklist with them, and explain the actor's process in more detail. There are twelve in this group, and since they are not particularly self-sufficient, I help them assign the tasks from the worklist. I divide them into three smaller groups of four each. All three subgroups will search for and record character evidence in the text about the narrator, the girl, and the saleslady. The first subgroup will also write a one-page biography for each character; they may do this work as a group or split the characters among themselves. The second subgroup will write about the relationships between the characters, again either as a group or by splitting the characters among themselves. The third subgroup will identify and write about any time gaps in the poem and write a description of what they think happens before the poem begins and after it ends. I make sure that all students know exactly what they are responsible for accomplishing and tell them that they have the rest of this class period to do the work and can finish anything they do not complete as homework. I also remind them that they need to select three members of the group to portray the characters when we enact the poem tomorrow.

### First Consultation with the Designers

I next consult with the group of designers, explain their process in more detail, review the tasks on their worklist, and answer any questions. I remind the designers that today they will accomplish the preparation work and tomorrow they will create an environment for "Oranges" in the classroom. Dividing this group of twelve into three groups of four, I ask each subgroup to read the text and find all of the explicit and implicit information they can about the context. I remind them that they can write notes on their copy of the text or take separate notes as they read (see Figures 8.1 and 8.2). They must define what spaces are needed to tell the story, envision the environment for the poem in the classroom, and draw a sketch of it.

Each subgroup also needs to create a list of props needed for the story. When each subgroup has sketched out its vision, they will all share with each other, and I will help them decide on one design. I will then bring them together to collaborate with the directors to make sure their environment will accommodate the action of the poem. With the directors, we will decide on one design to build tomorrow in the classroom and make a sketch of it today before we leave class.

### First Consultation with the Directors

I consult next with the group of directors, explain the director's process in more detail, and go over their worklist with them. Defining both physical and verbal action, I tell the directors they must read the poem to find the action that tells the story and make a list of the sequence of actions. Once they have their list of actions, they need to start at the end of the list and verify that each action has been motivated by the previous one. I divide the group of eleven directors into three smaller groups to find the poem's actions. Once each subgroup has generated a list of actions, they will compare the results and integrate them into one list of actions for the poem from beginning to end. I remind them that I

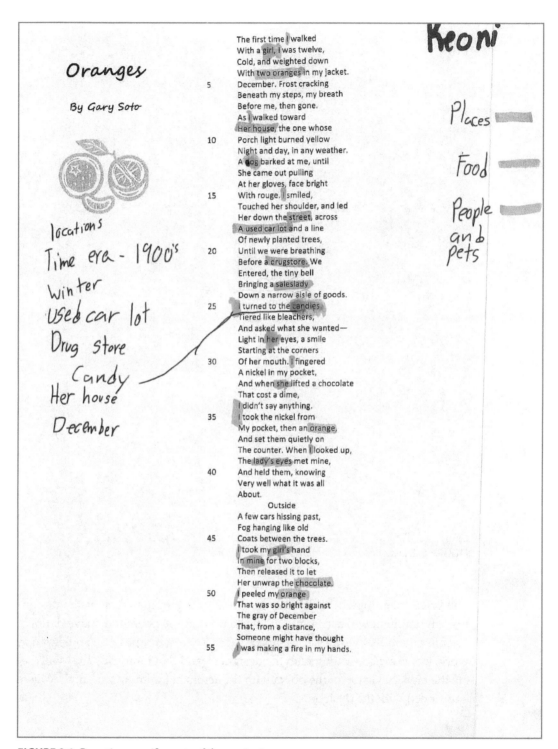

**FIGURE 8.1.** Denoting specific parts of the content.

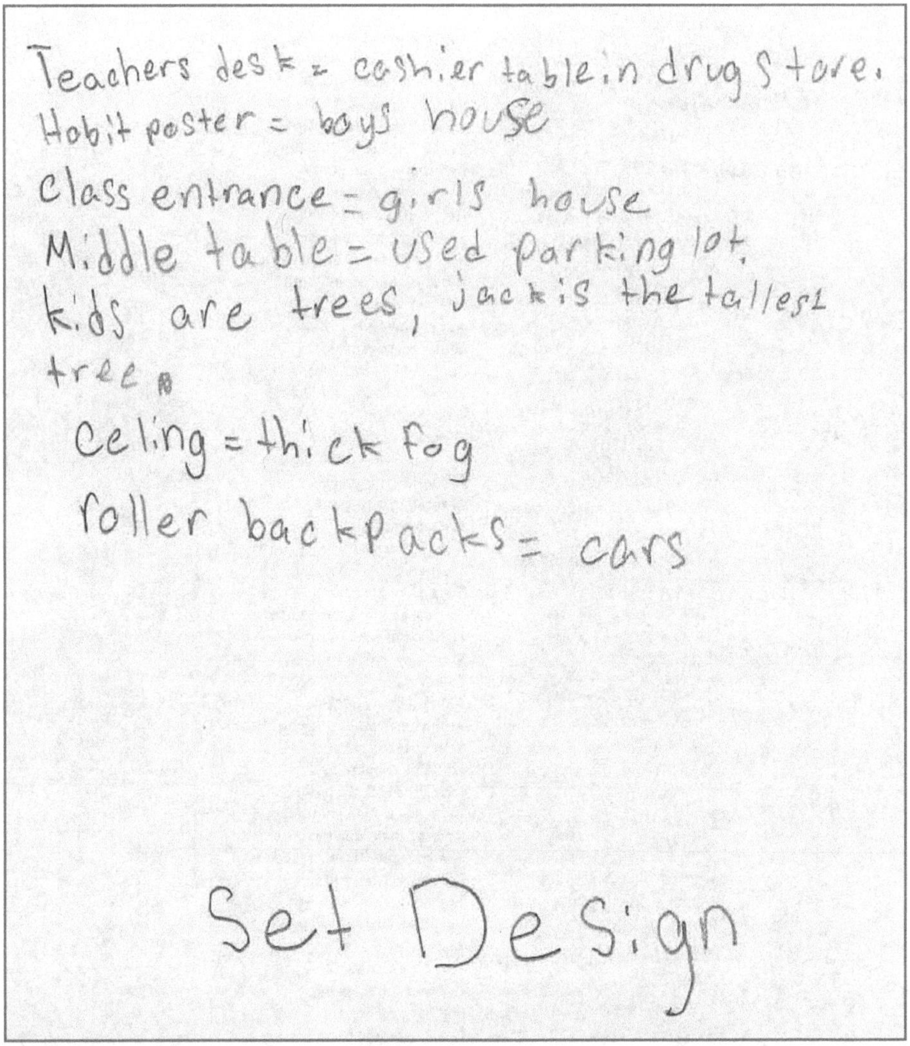

Teachers desk = cashier table in drug Store.
Hobit poster = boys house
Class entrance = girls house
Middle table = Used parking lot,
kids are trees, jack is the tallest
tree.
  Celing = thick fog
  roller backpacks = cars



Set Design

**FIGURE 8.2.** List of context elements for a set design.

will bring them together with the designers to determine whether the designers' environment will accommodate the actions of the poem they have defined. I remind them that today's class time is set aside to accomplish this preparation work, including consulting with the designers, and that tomorrow they will create the physical action of the poem with the actors in the environment they have envisioned with the designers.

## WORKING INDEPENDENTLY

After I have consulted with each group, I let the groups work independently, and each one continues its process of searching the text for information and then using it to accomplish its assigned tasks. The actors work to find evidence to create characters' biographies and relationships and fill in time gaps. The designers search the text for evidence of context and envision what it will look like, and the directors delve into the text to find the poem's sequence of actions. I keep a close eye on the clock so that we will finish all of the preparation work in today's class session.

## SECOND CONSULTATION WITH THE DESIGNERS

I visit the group of designers first this time to help them develop the environment. They tell me they have discovered that the poem needs three physical spaces: the girl's house, the drugstore, and a path to walk between them. They show me some rough sketches illustrating possible arrangements of the classroom (e.g., Figure 8.3) but say they haven't decided on one yet. I prompt them to consider what is between the girl's house and the drugstore (i.e., to find it in the text) and how much space the characters need to accomplish any action that occurs while they walk. I also ask them to consider what has to happen inside the drugstore (find it in the text) and what furniture they need to accommodate that action. I tell them to think again about the space with these considerations in mind, and I will be back shortly to see what they have decided and to bring them together with the directors, who will want to verify that the space can accommodate the action.

## SECOND CONSULTATION WITH THE DIRECTORS

Next, I check in with the directors to see if they have generated the poem's sequence of actions and verified them for continuity. They are in the process of sharing the actions each group has found (see Figures 8.4 and 8.5). Reminding them they need to think about the space for these actions and how the classroom can be reconfigured to accommodate the action of the poem, I tell them I will be back shortly to bring them together with the designers to coordinate their ideas.

## SECOND CONSULTATION WITH THE ACTORS

I confer again with the actors and find that they have finished their search of the text and listed what the writer has stated about the characters (see Figure 8.6). They are now inferring from the text to create the characters' biographies and relationships (see Figure 8.7). They found only one small period of time not accounted for in the poem, and they are concentrating on creating the action that

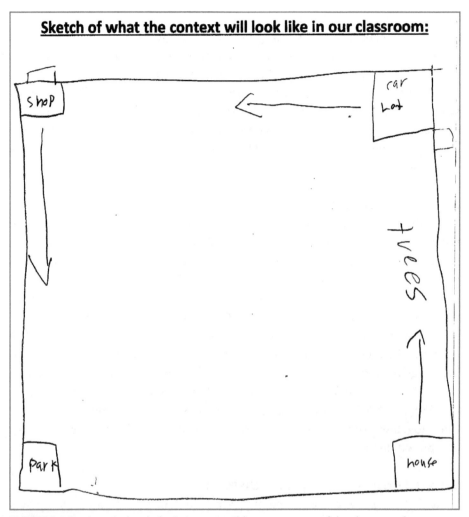

**Sketch of what the context will look like in our classroom:**

shop

car Lot

trees

park

house

**FIGURE 8.3.** Designer's sketch depicting a possible arrangement of the classroom for "Oranges."

occurs before the poem begins and after it ends. I remind them that they need to have the written biographies, character relationships, and accounts of "before and after" the poem by tomorrow—anything they don't finish by the end of class, they may finish as homework. They also need to decide who will enact the characters of the narrator, the girl, and the saleslady tomorrow. I make sure all members of the group know what they are responsible for having ready by tomorrow. They get back to work on their writing.

**WORKSHEET 8**

Literary Work: _Oranges_

Directors: Evelyn, Roman, Sammy, Julian

Character: **The Boy**

| Physical Action | Verbal Action |
|---|---|
| I walked | HE asked what she wanted |
| I walked toward her house | |
| I touched her shoulder ad led Her down the street. | |
| turned to the candies | |
| smile from the corner of her eye | |
| | |
| | |
| | |
| | |
| | |
| | |

**FIGURE 8.4.** Worksheet recording physical and verbal action.

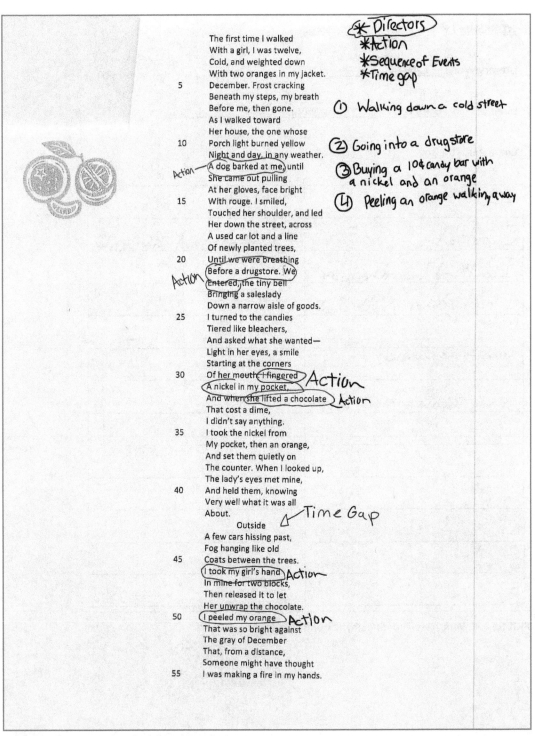

The first time I walked
With a girl, I was twelve,
Cold, and weighted down
With two oranges in my jacket.
5   December. Frost cracking
Beneath my steps, my breath
Before me, then gone.
As I walked toward
Her house, the one whose
10   Porch light burned yellow
Night and day, in any weather.
Action — A dog barked at me, until
She came out pulling
At her gloves, face bright
15   With rouge. I smiled,
Touched her shoulder, and led
Her down the street, across
A used car lot and a line
Of newly planted trees,
20   Until we were breathing
Action   Before a drugstore. We
Entered, the tiny bell
Bringing a saleslady
Down a narrow aisle of goods.
25   I turned to the candies
Tiered like bleachers,
And asked what she wanted—
Light in her eyes, a smile
Starting at the corners
30   Of her mouth. I fingered   Action
A nickel in my pocket,
And when she lifted a chocolate   Action
That cost a dime,
I didn't say anything.
35   I took the nickel from
My pocket, then an orange,
And set them quietly on
The counter. When I looked up,
The lady's eyes met mine,
40   And held them, knowing
Very well what it was all
About.   ← Time Gap
Outside
A few cars hissing past,
Fog hanging like old
45   Coats between the trees.
I took my girl's hand   Action
In mine for two blocks,
Then released it to let
Her unwrap the chocolate.
50   I peeled my orange   Action
That was so bright against
The gray of December
That, from a distance,
Someone might have thought
55   I was making a fire in my hands.

Handwritten margin notes:

* Directors
* Action
* Sequence of Events
* Time gap

(1) Walking down a cold street

(2) Going into a drugstore

(3) Buying a 10¢ candy bar with a nickel and an orange

(4) Peeling an orange walking away

**FIGURE 8.5.** Actions identified directly on the text.

**WORKSHEET 5:**

Literary Work _____ Oranges _____

Actors: _____ Dog, girl, boy, Saleslady _____

Character Biography: **The Boy**

| Date and Place of Birth/Age in Story | 12 years old , 2005, December 5 |
| --- | --- |
| Parents | He does |
| Siblings | No |
| Childhood Memories | He walked with a girl for the first time |
| Education | He knows what a dime and nickel is |
| Work History | In the past 1950. |
| Important Relationships | He has a girlfriend |
| Significant Life events | |

**FIGURE 8.6.** Textual information recorded on a worksheet to help create a character biography.

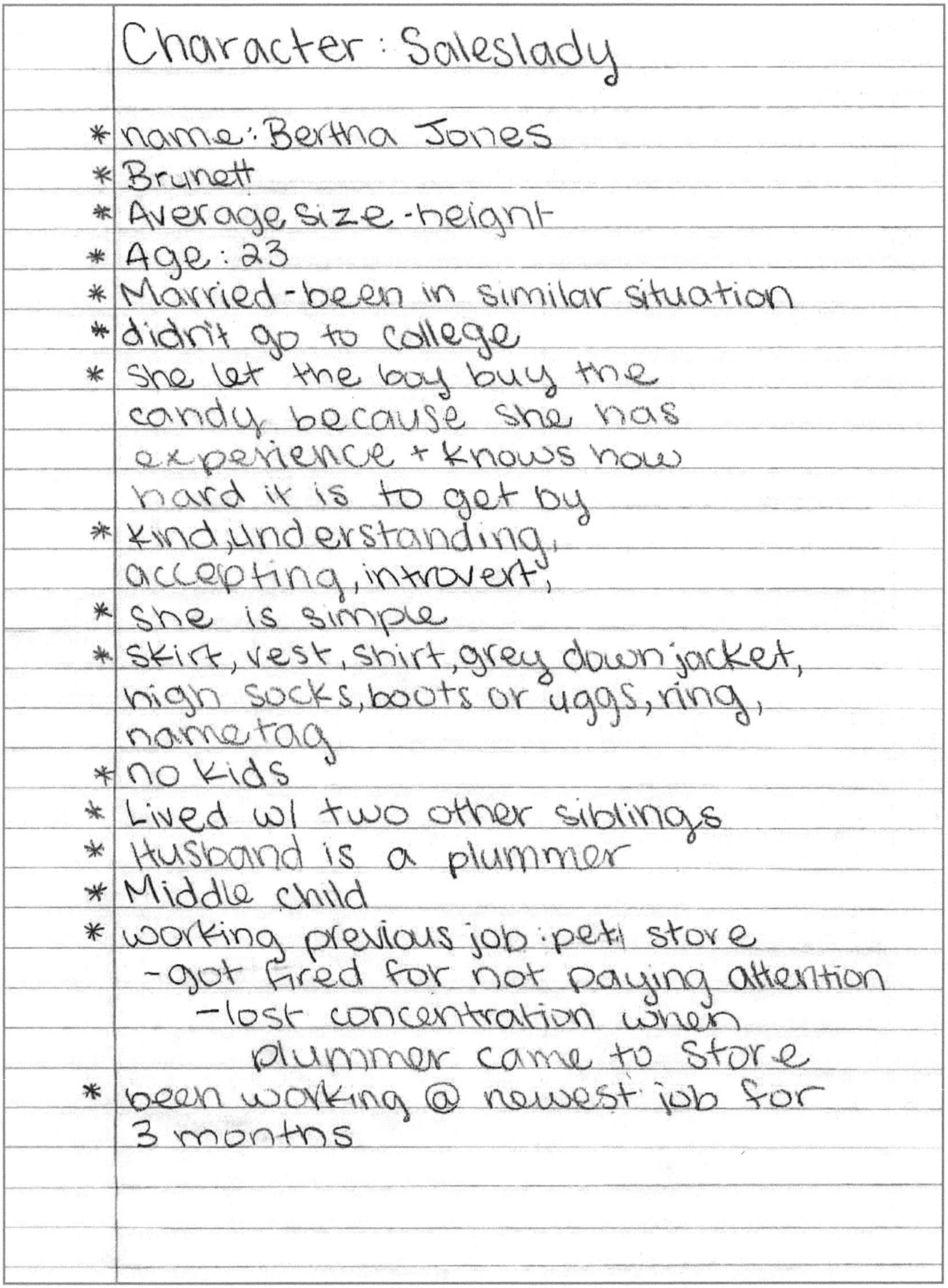

## Character: Saleslady

* name: Bertha Jones
* Brunett
* Average size - height
* Age: 23
* Married - been in similar situation
* didn't go to college
* She let the boy buy the candy because she has experience + knows how hard it is to get by
* kind, understanding, accepting, introvert,
* she is simple
* skirt, vest, shirt, grey down jacket, high socks, boots or uggs, ring, name tag
* no kids
* Lived w/ two other siblings
* Husband is a plummer
* Middle child
* working previous job: pet store
  - got fired for not paying attention
    - lost concentration when plummer came to store
* been working @ newest job for 3 months

**FIGURE 8.7.** Preliminary list of character traits for use in writing a character biography of the saleslady.

## Step 2. Designers and Directors Collaborate to Envision the Context and Action

I then bring the designers and directors together for collaboration. The designers show the directors their rough sketch and explain how they want to rearrange the classroom to create the environment for "Oranges." The designers have placed the girl's house at one corner of the room and the drugstore at an adjacent corner. The directors want more space between the girl's house and the drugstore since they think that "A used car lot" and "a line / Of newly planted trees" would take up a lot of space. The designers suggest placing the drugstore diagonally across the room from the girl's house to create more walking space, and the directors agree. As they discuss this idea of space, I watch their thinking process change from the generic notion that the characters go to the drugstore to deliberation about the specifics of the text.

The directors also tell the designers that they think the girl and the narrator walk in the opposite direction from the girl's house when they leave the drugstore, but the designers think they walk the earlier route back to her house. The students discuss the two options and ultimately decide to have the pair walk back to the girl's house. To make this decision, students looked back at the text and discovered that when the pair leaves the drugstore, they are confronted with "A few cars hissing past, / Fog hanging like old / Coats between the trees." The students decide that the cars are being test driven from the used car lot. Thus, once again, they have reread the text and found additional meaning between the lines to justify their decision.

I now verify that the designers have a detailed sketch of what we have decided on (Figure 8.8) and that the directors have their sequence of actions ready for tomorrow. I also remind the directors that they must choose someone to be the reader when we do the enactment tomorrow. I remind the designers about the props, and they designate who will bring in what props for tomorrow. You can assume the responsibility of bringing in the props or have the designers take responsibility for it.

Having completed our preliminary work, the actors, designers, and directors know what they need to complete as homework to be ready to build the environment and enact the poem tomorrow.

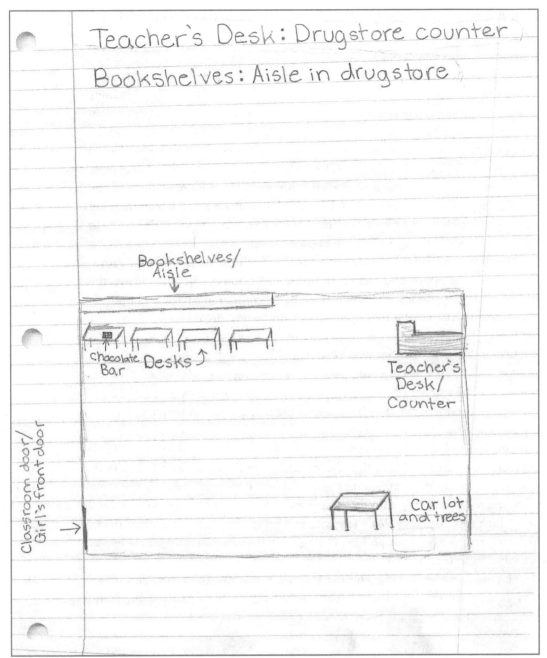

**FIGURE 8.8.** Classroom configuration agreed on by directors and designers for "Oranges."

## Day Two

### Step 3. Directors, Designers, and Actors Collaborate to Create the Enactment in the Context

As students come into the room on day two, they immediately get into their groups and check that they have everything ready for today's work. While the actors and directors are finishing their preparation, I meet with the designers, ask them to refer to the sketch they made yesterday, and start the process of reconfiguring the classroom to create the environment for "Oranges." Trying not to completely disrupt the work of the actors and directors, we move desks to create a walking path between the two diagonal corners of the room and relocate a table and a bookshelf into the one corner to represent the drugstore counter and the candy display. The students make sure there is enough space in front of the counter for the girl and the narrator and behind it for the saleslady. They place some books on top of the bookshelf and set out the candies so they are "Tiered like bleachers." They place two model cars they have brought in and a potted plant in one corner of the room to represent the "used car lot and line / Of newly planted trees."

I now bring the actors and directors together with the designers and have the designers explain the environment to everyone. They show the actors and directors where the girl's house and the drugstore are and define the walking path through the used car lot and line of trees between them. In consultation with the directors, they decide to move the model cars and the potted plant representing the used car lot a little closer to the center of the room to create a better walking area. They define the space in front of and behind the counter in the drugstore and explain that when the narrator and the girl leave the drugstore, they will walk the same path back to the girl's house. One of the actors asks where the saleslady is when the narrator and the girl walk into the drugstore, and the designers designate an area along the wall where the saleslady can be before she hears the bell ("the tiny bell / Bringing a saleslady / Down a narrow aisle of goods"). I ask the designers to place all of the props in their proper locations in the environment. Having already set up the candies, they place two oranges and a nickel in the jacket they have brought for the narrator and place the gloves at the girl's house. They give the bell to a member of their own group, who will ring it when the narrator and the girl enter the drugstore so the saleslady knows they are there.

I ask if everyone is ready to start the enactment of the poem and remind them that our enactment is not for an audience but to help us see the story of the poem. I ask which actors are playing the roles and ask the directors to place the characters where they would be before the action begins. I remind the actors not to bring their copies of the text, so they can concentrate on creating the characters' actions and listen to the directions given to them by the directors. The directors confer with the actors and decide that the narrator is in the kitchen at home taking two oranges off of the counter and the girl is at her house putting on rouge and talking to the dog. The directors give the narrator the jacket but take the oranges and the nickel out of the pockets, saying that the narrator doesn't have them yet. In consultation with the designers, we place the narrator's house on the opposite side of the room from the girl's house. The director who has been designated as reader begins to read the poem, and we start.

The directors tell the narrator to pick up the oranges, put one in each jacket pocket, walk back into the bedroom to get the nickel and put it in a pocket, and start to walk toward the girl's house. As the narrator gets close to the girl's house, one of the directors, representing the dog, barks. The directors remind the girl to put her gloves on as she comes out of the door to meet the narrator. Per the poem, the directors coach the narrator to smile, touch the girl's shoulder, and lead her down the street toward the drugstore. The actors ask how close together they should walk, and the directors tell them side by side. I stop the action and ask if there's any dialogue here. They all refer back to the text and realize there is not. I ask how the girl and the narrator are communicating if there is no dialogue, and the directors respond that the communication has to happen through physical actions, such as the narrator touching her shoulder, walking close to her, and smiling at her. The directors coach them in these actions and guide them to walk "across / A used car lot and a line / Of newly planted trees."

When the narrator and the girl reach the drugstore, the designer with the bell rings it, and the directors remind the saleslady to move down the wall to her place behind the counter to greet them. The directors ask the narrator to create some dialogue by asking the girl if she wants a candy. The girl selects a chocolate and puts it on the counter. I ask where the girl should go after this, and the directors tell her to move away from the counter so that the narrator and the saleslady can more clearly see each other. The directors then tell the narrator to place one orange and the nickel on the counter, look at the saleslady, realize that she will accept this as payment, pick up the candy, and walk out the door with the girl.

## Delving Deeper: Finding More Meaning

At this point, I stop the action to guide students toward a deeper understanding of what is happening in the poem. I first ask the designers if they think the environment is accommodating the action. They think it is but decide that the counter in the drugstore is too close to the wall and doesn't allow the narrator and the saleslady enough space for the action that has to occur between them about the payment. I ask them why they want to create more space there and they say that the silent interaction between the narrator and the saleslady is important to the story and should have sufficient space in which to occur. We all agree, and the designers move the counter farther from the wall.

I then ask the actors what is going on between the girl and the narrator at this moment in the poem. They confer, and the actor portraying the girl decides she sees a game set she has wanted across the aisle and goes to look at it. The directors like this idea because it gets the girl out of the way so that the important action can occur between the saleslady and the narrator. I ask what the narrator feels at this moment, and the narrator admits being nervous about not having enough money to pay for the chocolate the girl has selected and not knowing what to do. The narrator recalls once seeing someone pay for something at the hardware store with a basket of fruit and decides to try it. The narrator places the nickel and the orange on the counter and begs the saleslady with a pleading look to accept this offering as payment.

Focusing my comments to the directors, I ask them how the narrator will know whether the saleslady accepts the offer of payment since there is no dialogue. They decide that the saleslady should give the narrator a nod of her head when she makes her decision. The directors ask the saleslady what she is thinking when the narrator places the orange and the nickel on the counter. She says that the narrator seems so sincere and so sweet with the girl that she decides she will accept the payment. The directors tell the actor playing the narrator not to exhale until the saleslady makes her decision and nods her head. The directors then tell the narrator to pick up the chocolate, hand it to the girl, and lead her out the door. One of the designers rings the bell again as they exit.

One of the directors then wants to try it another way, having the girl select the chocolate and stay right next to the narrator at the counter and watch while the narrator tries to pay for it. The narrator looks at the girl, trying not to give away the fact that there isn't enough money to pay for the candy. As she watches, the directors ask what the narrator is thinking, and the narrator describes feeling embarrassed, not knowing what to do, and puts both hands in the jacket pockets to keep them from shaking. There, the narrator finds the oranges and, not knowing what else to do, places one orange and the nickel on the counter and silently prays that the saleslady will accept this payment for the chocolate. The saleslady and the girl both look on as the narrator suffers in silence, and finally the saleslady gives the narrator a nod and accepts the payment. The narrator then quickly picks up the candy and gives it to the girl, and they exit the drugstore.

We go back and reenact both of these options and compare them. We talk about how having both the girl and the saleslady watch while the narrator agonizes about how to pay for the candy adds more tension to the moment. Some think it puts too much strain on the narrator and feel that the story is communicated more effectively if the girl isn't watching. The actors talk about what the different options reveal about the characters, and the directors debate which action choice best builds to the climax of the poem. Comparing these options leads us to a fruitful discussion of how actions and space can tell a story, especially when there is no dialogue. We finally decide that moving the girl away helps focus the attention on what is happening between the narrator and the saleslady, and since that dynamic is more important to the story, we settle on this option.

Now one of the directors wants to try something else, suggesting we add a new character to the enactment—namely, an older narrator standing at the side of the action, watching the younger self go through it, and remembering what it was like. The actors and directors like this idea because it provides another visual stimulus to tell the story. If we add the older narrator, we not only see the story that is happening but also watch the older version of the character observe the younger self and remember what that self learned from this moment in life. One of the actors comes in to represent our newly created character, and the designers find a special spot for the character to stand and watch. They like this idea so much that they now want to go back to the beginning and start the action again with the older narrator reliving the whole story. We restart from the beginning and realize how much the character watching adds to the significance of the story. The directors decide that the older narrator should not only watch the story but also react to what is happening, adding another layer of meaning to the poem as it unfolds. Note that this older narrator is not indicated explicitly in Gary Soto's poem but came entirely from the readers' work of building on the text with their own imaginations, thus illustrating how the reading process facilitates readers' interaction with the text, discovery of meaning, and creation of ways to express it.

When we get to the end of the enactment, the directors ask why the narrator thought the orange against the grey sky looked like fire, and the narrator describes realizing how lucky it was to escape an embarrassing situation and how good it felt that the girl never knew what was happening. Asked the same question, the older narrator admits thinking about how lucky he had been in that moment, but, looking back on it, says that it represents the younger self's feelings for the girl, as the two later married each other.

This method of stopping the action and engaging in inquiry with your students as actors, designers, and directors creates an exceptional learning opportunity. While the enactment in the environment gives readers a way to see the story, stopping the action and examining alternative possibilities allows them to find meaning in multiple ways, and engaging with the literature in their roles as actors, designers, and directors gives them agency in the meaning-making process.

Not wanting to miss a good opportunity, I give a writing assignment for homework. I ask the students to write one page on the following question: What did you discover about the structure and the meaning of the poem "Oranges" from the point of view of an actor, a designer, or a director? What did you learn from the other artists who helped you transform the written poem into an experience?

# Students Collaborate on "Thank You, M'am"

## *Day One*

I start the process for "Thank You, M'am" in a similar way, by telling the students we are going to do something very different with what we are reading today and tomorrow. I tell them we will read the short story "Thank You, M'am," and I share with them some background on the story and on writer Langston Hughes.

I tell them we are going to read the short story together once "as ourselves," but then we will try a different reading process. I explain that we are going to borrow some reading techniques from the world of the theater, because theater artists read in a unique way so they can create a representation of the text's characters, context, and action for the stage. I assure them that we will *not* be creating a stage production for an audience but will create an environment for the story and generate its action in the classroom.

We then read the short story aloud as a class. I tell them that when we read the story again, we will no longer be reading as ourselves but will engage in a little role-playing. Some of them will read as actors, searching the text for character information, creating biographies of the characters, defining their relationships, and filling in any time gaps in the story. Some of them will read as designers, searching the text to find evidence of the story's context and envisioning what it will look like in order to build it in the classroom. And some will read as directors, searching the text for evidence of the story's action, creating how the action will be represented, and generating an enactment of it in the classroom.

I tell the students that I will be the producer to help them accomplish their goals and collaborate so that we can create the story's characters in action in an environment. I explain that we will accomplish this process over the course of two class periods, using today for preparation work and tomorrow for constructing the environment and enacting the story.

They think I have lost my mind but are willing to try it.

## Step 1. Divide the Class into Three Groups and Assign Each Group a Worklist

I divide the class into three groups, designating who will be actors, who will be designers, and who will be directors. I distribute the appropriate worklists to each group—the same ones used for the collaborative reading of "Oranges"— and ask them to notice that each worklist begins with a search to find specific information in the text. They should all now start with that reading step and take notes, either writing on the text or on a separate paper or typing on a laptop (see Figures 8.9 and 8.10), while I come around to consult with each group and explain their process in more detail. Thus we begin our collaborative process.

| WORKSHEET 7: | | |
|---|---|---|

**Literary Work:** Thank You, Ma'am

**Actors:** _____

**Time Gaps**

| Time Gap in story or before or after | Amount of Time | What happens |
|---|---|---|
| Roger Looking at Blue suede shoes | 20 secs | walks down road thinking how he would get the shoes |
| Mrs. Jones at work closing the Shop finishing customer | 5 minutes | last customer closes shop and starts walking home |
| Roger runs to the shop to get shoes finds out its closed | 2 minutes | runs to the store and sees that its closed |

**FIGURE 8.9.** Worksheet for thinking through short time gaps in the story line.

**Written account of what occurs before the story begins:**

Roger walks to store and looks at shoes in the
~~shopping~~ store window. He leaves pondering how he
will get the money. Mrs. Jones closes the
hair salon, as the last employee and
customer leaves.

**Written account of what occurs after the story ends:**

After Mrs. Jones closes the door
Roger runs to the store to find
that it is closed.

FIGURE 8.10. Worksheet for thinking through what happens before and after the story.

## FIRST CONSULTATION WITH THE ACTORS

This particular class is highly motivated. The group of eleven actors easily forms three subgroups and divides the tasks on the worklist. Establishing that there are no major internal time gaps in the story, we decide that one group will focus on Mrs. Jones, write her biography, and establish what she is doing before and after the story. The second group will concentrate on Roger, write his biography, and establish what he is doing before and after the story. And the third group will write about the characters' relationship, how it changes during the story, and why. I make sure they all know exactly what they are responsible for accomplishing and remind them that they have this class period to do the work and can finish anything they do not complete as homework. They also need to select two members of the group to portray the characters of Mrs. Jones and Roger when we enact the story tomorrow.

## FIRST CONSULTATION WITH THE DESIGNERS

Reviewing the worklist with the designers, I explain that they must search the text for evidence of context, then envision how we can reconfigure the classroom to represent an environment for "Thank You, M'am." I divide this group of ten designers into three smaller groups and ask each group to read the text, search for and record all the information they find about the context, and determine what spaces are needed for the story. Each group will then envision the environment of "Thank You, M'am," draw a sketch of how to rearrange the classroom to represent it, and create a list of props needed for the story. I tell them that when each group has decided on its vision and sketched it out, they will share them with each other and decide on one design. Later in today's class, I will bring them together with the directors to verify that the environment will accommodate all of the story's action (see Figure 8.11). After we collaborate with the directors, we will make any needed changes, decide on one design to create in the classroom tomorrow, and draw an accurate sketch of the design. We will also decide what props are needed and designate who will bring them in tomorrow.

## FIRST CONSULTATION WITH THE DIRECTORS

I consult with the group of eleven directors, reminding them they must find all of the action that happens in the text, create a sequential list of the actions, and verify that each action is motivated by the preceding one. I make sure to review both physical and verbal action with them. This group of self-motivated students agrees to work together as one group to determine the story's actions. I remind them that later in the class period I will bring them together with the designers who are creating the environment to determine whether the environment will accommodate the actions.

**WORKSHEET 4:**

Literary Work: _____ Thank You Ma'am _____

Set Designer(s): _____

| Important Action in the Story | Arrangement of the set to accommodate it |
|---|---|
| • He tries to steal her purse. He falls down. <br> • She picks him up & drags him around the corner & up the street. | • The alley is in between two tables nearest to the back door <br> • She drags him between the tables & the poster. <br> • The corner is by the stairs |
| • They enter the house <br> • He washes his face <br> • He sits on the day-bed and she gets the food | • Between counselor office and last table is hall of the house with other people <br> • There is a stool and a bowl for the sink where the cranberry is <br> • He sits on a couch while she goes behind the bookshelf |
| • They eat together and talk | • They sit in the chairs that are attached to the desks. Food & mugs are on the table |
| • She sends him out and says goodbye | • She lets him out the same way they came in |

**FIGURE 8.11.** Worksheet for determining how the set arrangement will accommodate the story's action.

## WORKING INDEPENDENTLY

I let the groups get to work, and each group continues its process of searching the text and finding evidence to use in accomplishing its tasks. The actors examine the text to find evidence on which to build the characters' lives, the designers search the text for evidence of context, and the directors investigate the text to find the story's sequence of actions (see Figure 8.12). I keep a close eye on the time so that we will finish all of the preparation work in today's class session.

**WORKSHEET 8**

Literary Work: Thank You, Ma'am

Directors: Lily, Rochel, Ava, lucky, Toni, Lily, Camilla, Mosa, Alex, Brooks
Matthew

Character: **Roger**

| Physical Action | Verbal Action |
|---|---|
| Ran | says, " Yes'm " |
| Stole a bag | asks Mrs. Jones to let him go |
| Falls | Blue svede shoes |
| Gets Hit | |
| Eat | |
| Gets Dragged | |
| | |
| | |
| | |
| | |
| | |
| | |

**FIGURE 8.12.** Worksheet for tracking actions.

## SECOND CONSULTATION WITH THE DESIGNERS

After giving the groups some time to work independently, I visit the group of designers first to help them develop the environment. They tell me the story needs two spaces: the street where the characters first meet and Mrs. Jones's boardinghouse room where she takes Roger. They realize they also need a substantial space for a walkway between the two locations because action and dialogue occur during the journey between the two spaces. They also notice that Mrs. Jones's room in the boardinghouse is cramped and contains a lot of furniture. They show me a sketch illustrating a possible arrangement of the classroom, using one corner of the room for the street where the characters meet and an adjacent corner of the room for Mrs. Jones's boardinghouse room, but they are not sure it will provide enough room for the action. I ask them to think again and consider if there is any other way to reconfigure the classroom to create more space for the action of the story. I tell them I will be back shortly to see what they have decided and to bring them together to collaborate with the directors.

## SECOND CONSULTATION WITH THE DIRECTORS

I check in with the directors to see if they have generated a sequence of actions, and they have. I ask if any of them know how to apply a half nelson. They realize they don't, so I demonstrate how to do it safely and tell them they will need to demonstrate this action to the actors tomorrow. Reminding them they also need to think about the spaces that the story's actions need, I tell them I will be back shortly to bring them together with the designers to share their ideas. The directors will need to consider the ideas the designers have created and collaborate with them to verify that the action of the story can be enacted in the space they have envisioned.

## SECOND CONSULTATION WITH THE ACTORS

I confer with the actors and find that they are on task. They have finished their search of the text and found what the writer has stated about the characters. They are now inferring from the text to create the characters' biographies and relationships (see Figure 8.13) and constructing what the characters are doing before the story begins and what they are thinking and doing after it ends. I remind them that they need to prepare the written biographies, character relationships, and accounts of before and after by tomorrow and that anything they don't finish by the end of class can be finished as homework. They also need to decide who among their group will enact the roles of Mrs. Jones and Roger tomorrow. They get back to work on their writing.

Written Account of the relationship between Mrs. Jones and Roger:

Mrs. Jones almost gets robbed by Roger, which makes her upset because he is disrespectful. But, then she discovers that he has a troubled home and feels empathy because she went through the same experience. They grow close at her house and develop a trusting relationship. Finally, when he leaves, they don't ever meet again. Throughout this story, Mrs. Jones has a clear maternal instinct over Roger.

**FIGURE 8.13.** Description of character relationship based on inferences from the text.

### Step 2. Designers and Directors Collaborate to Envision the Context and Action

I now bring the designers and directors together for collaboration. The designers show the directors their sketch and explain their idea of placing the street in one corner of the room and Mrs. Jones's boardinghouse room in an adjacent corner, but they wonder if this setup will give the actors enough space for their walk between the two locations. The directors refer back to the text and realize how much action occurs during the walk between the two spaces and don't think that arrangement will provide enough room. They all think about how they can create more space.

One of the directors suggests they put Mrs. Jones's boardinghouse room in the corner of the room that is diagonal to where the street is, which would create more room to walk. The designers like the idea, but the directors still wonder if it gives them enough space. At this point I am tempted to suggest using the periphery of the room as a walkway but decide to let them solve the problem themselves. One of the directors then suggests the characters could walk a zig-zag path across the center of the room to create more ground to cover. They all think this is a good solution and agree to go with it. You can decide how much you want to contribute to the collaboration and how much you want your students to solve problems for themselves. This decision will vary with the literature, the time you have, and the ability of your students.

Now we look at the corner of the room to decide if it will give us enough space for all of the furniture in Mrs. Jones's room and the action that needs to occur there. The designers look at their list of what needs to be in the room: daybed, sink, table and chairs, screen separating a small kitchenette with gas plate and icebox, ham, lima beans, pitcher or pot for cocoa, ten-cent cake, dishes, cups, silverware, and napkins. They look at the corner of the room and realize how small it is. One of the directors then suggests that the boardinghouse room could extend out into the center of the room from the corner to create more space, and they decide to try it.

They look around the room to see what they can use for the items in the boardinghouse room. This particular classroom lacks individual desks but has freestanding tables and chairs, which works to our advantage. The students decide to use two chairs to create the daybed and put two other chairs next to one of the smaller tables and turn a chair upside down to represent the sink. They spy a short bookcase in one corner of the room that can create a separation from the kitchenette and also be used as a place to store the dishes, cups, silverware, napkins, and food. They decide to use two chairs with books stacked on them to form a surface for the gas plate and icebox. We don't move any furniture yet but envision that all of this setup can fit in the corner if we allow her room to come out into the center space. This arrangement will also show how cramped the space is for Mrs. Jones. We will move the remaining tables and chairs over to the walls of the classroom to give us an open space in the middle of the room for the characters to walk through. The designers and directors look at each other and decide they will try it tomorrow, and if it doesn't work, they can make adjustments in the space. I make sure the designers create an accurate sketch of what they decide, and they consult the prop list and decide who will bring in which props tomorrow.

Before we leave for the day, I check with each group to make sure everyone knows what they need to have completed by tomorrow so that we will be ready to build the environment in the classroom and enact the story.

## Day Two

### Step 3. Directors, Designers, and Actors Collaborate to Create the Enactment in the Context

When the students come into the classroom on day two, they immediately settle into their groups. While the actors are sharing their written work with each other, I bring the designers and directors together to start the process of rearranging the classroom to create the environment for "Thank You, M'am." Referring back to the sketch we made yesterday, we move tables and chairs to create a space between the two diagonal corners of the room and begin the process of setting up Mrs. Jones's boardinghouse room in the corner and extending it out into the center of the classroom. Again consulting the sketch, we move two chairs into the space to serve as the daybed, place a small table and two chairs next to it, and turn over a chair to create a sink. We move the bookshelf to create the screen and build the surface for the gas plate and the icebox with two chairs and some books. Students pool the collection of props they have brought in and place them where they belong in the environment. They realize that all of this furniture in the space takes up more room than they had anticipated, but the directors think they will be able to make it work. The creation of the environment has clearly become a collaborative effort between the designers and the directors. The directors then show the actor playing Mrs. Jones how to hold the purse and explain how the strap of the purse can appear to break when Roger grabs it (see Figure 8.14).

I ask if everyone is ready to start the enactment and request that the actors playing Mrs. Jones and Roger come forward. I remind the two actors that they will not have the text in front of them, so they will have to listen to the directors to create the action of the story. I remind the directors they need to be very specific in their direction so the actors know what to do. I ask the actor playing

<u>**Sketch out a graphic depiction of the action of the Story:**</u>

**FIGURE 8.14.** Graphic depiction of the purse snatching.

Mrs. Jones where the character is before the action begins, and we agree she is coming home from work ("she told him about her job in a hotel beauty shop that stayed open late," and "It was about eleven o'clock at night"). I ask the actor playing Roger where his character is before the action begins. The text doesn't tell us, but the actor thinks Roger is sitting on the ground near an intersection waiting for someone to come along who has a purse he can snatch to get money to buy the blue suede shoes he wants. I ask what Roger is doing out in the street so late, and the actor says the text reveals that no one is at home at his house. With these answers, the actors validate that they had found information in the text to develop the specifics of their characters' lives. The directors place Mrs. Jones on the opposite side of the room so she can walk past Roger, whom they place sitting on the floor in the corner of the room.

The director selected to read the story begins, and the directors ask Mrs. Jones to walk right by Roger. They then coach the two characters through the actions as Roger gets up, grabs Mrs. Jones's purse, and falls down. Mrs. Jones then kicks him in the seat, picks him up by the shirtfront, and shakes him. The directors prompt the actors with dialogue as well. A few of the actors then also step into the action ("two or three people passed, stopped, turned to look, and some stood watching").

When we get to the dialogue where Mrs. Jones says, "Then it will get washed this evening," the directors tell her to start dragging Roger down the street toward her boardinghouse; they also tell the onlookers to disappear down the street. The directors coach Mrs. Jones to zigzag across the center of the room as if she is walking on a winding street to create more space for her to walk. She does so, dragging Roger behind her by the shirtfront, as the directors give them the dialogue. When Mrs. Jones says, "When I get through with you, sir, you are going to remember Mrs. Luella Bates Washington Jones," the directors show the actor how to safely put a half nelson around Roger's neck. She does so and drags him the rest of the way to the boardinghouse.

### Delving Deeper: Finding More Meaning

At this point, I stop the action and ask the actor playing Roger what the character is thinking. He admits having thought she was going to take him to the police station. Now, as they move in the opposite direction from the station, he thinks she might be taking him somewhere else and is wondering why. Once Mrs. Jones gets Roger to her boardinghouse room, the directors tell Mrs. Jones to ask his name, tell him to "go to that sink to wash your face," and finally release him from the half nelson.

I stop the action again to focus attention on the significance of what is happening at this moment in the story. I ask the actors, directors, and designers to look at the described action: "Roger looked at the door—looked at the woman— looked at the door—*and went to the sink*" (see Figure 8.15). I ask them to think about what is happening here. The directors think that Roger has an important decision to make: whether he will stay or run away while he has the chance. We look at options for where to place the characters to help use physical actions to tell the story. We put Mrs. Jones in front of the door and Roger farther into

**Write out a narrative description of the story's action**

Roger tries to steal Mrs. Jones's purse, but he falls. She scolds him and drags him to her house. She makes him wash his face and gives him food. She also gives Roger $10 to buy shoes and lets him go.

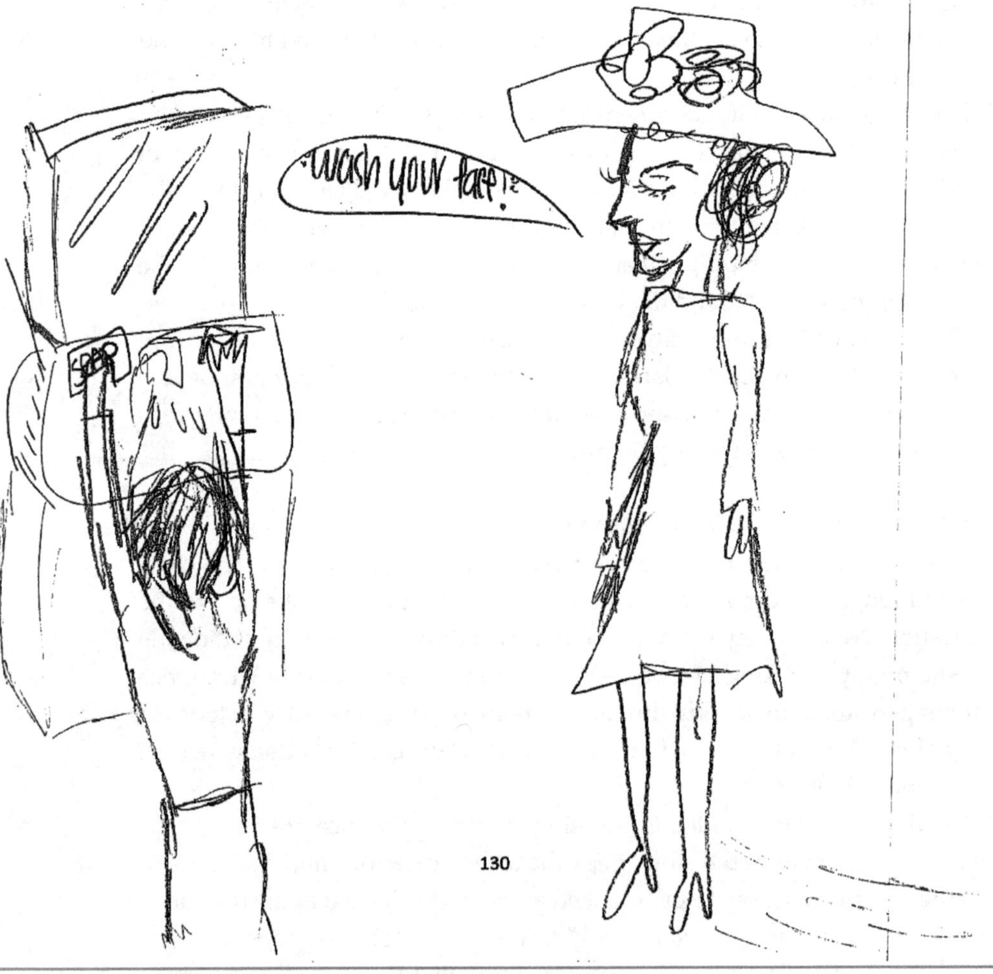


130

**FIGURE 8.15.** Directors' use of narrative and graphics to describe the story's action.

the room, near the sink, so that Mrs. Jones is physically blocking the door to keep Roger from running away. Some of the directors like this option because it shows how Mrs. Jones continues to use physical intimidation to control Roger's actions. Then we try moving Mrs. Jones to the other side of the sink, farther into the room, so there is nothing between Roger and the door, which gives him a clear path if he wants to run. Other directors like this option since it shows that Mrs. Jones is beginning to trust Roger.

The directors compare and discuss the two options and the implied meaning of each one. They realize that if there is a clear path between Roger and the door, we can see Roger think about running and then deciding to stay in order to show Mrs. Jones his good side. However, most of the directors think Mrs. Jones is not yet ready to trust Roger and physically blocks the doorway to prevent him from running away, so we ultimately choose that option. The process has given us the opportunity to closely examine this part of the story, compare choices, and discover how to use physical action and placement of characters to help tell the story. We comment on how much of the meaning we have unpacked by being able to experiment with this particular action and decide how representing it expresses its significance.

The directors coach Roger to wash his face at the sink and continue to prompt the actors with the dialogue. I stop the action again and point out the writer's inclusion of pauses ("a long pause. A very long pause," and shortly thereafter, "another long pause"). I ask the directors what they think is going on during these long pauses and how they can express what is happening through the action. They talk among themselves and speculate that Roger is again thinking about running away. They ask the actor playing Roger why he doesn't run this time. He thinks about it and admits that when Mrs. Jones says, "I were young once and I wanted things I could not get," he is interested in hearing her story and is grateful she is finally being nice to him. The students realize the importance of the pauses as a way to express that Roger needs time to think and make decisions, and that both characters are using the time to assess each other. The directors move Mrs. Jones away from the door when she feels she can trust that Roger won't run away.

We continue the action. This time the directors themselves stop the action because they realize the text tells them something important: "the boy took care to sit on the far side of the room, away from the purse, where he thought she could easily see him out of the corner of her eye if she wanted to." The directors discover that they can't accomplish this action with the furniture in its current arrangement. With the designers, they figure out how to move the angle of the bookcase acting as the screen so that Mrs. Jones can just see Roger sitting on one of the chairs when she is in the kitchenette. This leads us to a productive discussion about the characters' relationship at this point in the story. Although each is still cautious about the other, they are coming to trust each other a little more. Roger sits in a deliberately chosen spot: "He did not trust the woman not to trust him. And he did not want to be mistrusted now." Roger makes a decision here to sit away from the purse in a place where Mrs. Jones can see him so that he can prove himself trustworthy. The actor playing Roger notes that he even asks her, "Do you need somebody to go to the store . . . maybe to get some milk or something?" to show her how cooperative he can be.

It is certainly okay to change the arrangement of the environment during the enactment. Students are making new discoveries as they enact the story, and if they realize that they need to change the placement of something to accommodate the story's action, they are using their discoveries to understand the story at a deeper level and more accurately express its meaning.

The directors then coach Mrs. Jones through preparing the ham and lima beans and bringing two plates to the table. The designers have brought in a couple of pieces of bread and a few cheese cubes as props to represent the ham and lima beans, as well as a nutrition bar to represent the ten-cent cake. They ask the characters to improvise the dialogue at the table in order to play out the scene described in the story: "The woman did not ask the boy anything about where he lived, or his folks, or anything else that would embarrass him. Instead, as they ate, she told him about her job in a hotel beauty shop that stayed open late, what the work was like, and how all kinds of women came in and out. . . . Then she cut him a half of her ten-cent cake." We talk about how much each of them eats and decide Mrs. Jones probably eats very little because she wants to be sure Roger has enough, and she is also talking a lot. The actor playing Roger enjoys eating while listening to her.

Moving on to the enactment of the last actions of the story, the directors coach Mrs. Jones to go over to the daybed and direct her to take the money out of her purse to give Roger while she reminds him to behave himself: "Now here, take this ten dollars and buy yourself some blue suede shoes. And next time, do not make the mistake of latching onto *my* pocketbook *nor nobody else's*—because shoes got by devilish ways will burn your feet. I got to get my rest now. But from here on in, son, I hope you will behave yourself." The directors note that this dialogue helps place the story in the past because they have never heard the expression "shoes got by devilish ways will burn your feet."

The directors now tell Mrs. Jones to lead Roger to the door. They ask the actors what they have envisioned as the "after" action of the story since that was one of the actors' tasks. After listening to the actors' suggestions and comparing them, they ask Roger to walk a few steps away from the door, then turn back and look at Mrs. Jones, taking the time to think about what she has done for him by being kind, sharing a moment of her life with him, and not reporting him to the police. Creating this last moment in the story leads to a discussion about what each character is thinking at this point. It also prompts discussion of how each character has changed because of the events of the story, and students note how this last sequence of actions builds to a climax and leads us to see a change in each character. The actor playing Roger says that through the physical enactment of the whole story, he now realizes that Roger starts out needy and desperate as he tries to snatch the purse, then is terrified as Mrs. Jones physically intimidates and coerces him, and eventually feels grateful that she is so kind to him. The directors ask Roger to look at Mrs. Jones silently, start to walk away, and then turn back one more time and try to say thank you, only to see Mrs. Jones close the door. They think this additional action helps define how touched he is by her kindness. The actor playing Roger says this action gives him time to think about all that she has done for him.

We try some other options the actors have suggested for the action after the story. The directors try having Mrs. Jones close the door and then clear the table while Roger stays in the same spot staring at the door. We also try having Mrs. Jones close the door and stand near it to see if she can hear what Roger does, while Roger runs away. We decide that action doesn't express the right message. We ultimately settle on having Mrs. Jones close the door after Roger tries to say thank you, then clear the table and lie down on the daybed. Meanwhile Roger stares at the door and softly says, "Thank you, M'am," revealing his new-found respect for Mrs. Jones. One director suggests that Roger turn and walk a few more feet, stop again to look back and stare at the door once again, thinking about what he has learned, and then walk away. We find it interesting to simultaneously see the actions of both characters, knowing each one cannot see or hear the other, yet realizing how their actions have affected each other. We decide this visual action reinforces the ending of the story in the right way. None of this action is specified in the text, but it demonstrates how students have built on the text to further clarify the story's meaning and express it through action.

I have made sure to leave enough time at the end of the class period to restore the room to its original condition, and I now give this group of readers a written homework assignment. I ask them to write one page on the following question: From your perspective as an actor, designer, or director, how did this process help you understand the meaning of Langston Hughes's story "Thank You, M'am"?

## Collaborating with Novels

Using the collaborative process as a whole to construct and enact an entire novel is a bit overwhelming, but using parts of the process can be useful to help readers comprehend the complexity and continuity of novels. To that end, you can use any of the ideas described for "Oranges" and "Thank You, M'am," and here are some additional suggestions to focus reading on the discovery of character, context, and action in a collaborative way in the study of a novel.

1. Divide the class into groups of three with each group composed of an actor, a designer, and a director. Give each group a different scene from the novel. Ask the actors to trace the characters' journey from the beginning of the scene to the end and demonstrate how the characters are different at the end than they were at the beginning. Ask the designers to create the environment and make a sketch of it, and ask the directors to write out the sequence of actions in the scene.

2. Using the same framework (groups of three with one actor, one designer, and one director each), ask each group to build the environment and enact the scene for the rest of the class. You may need to add more actors to each group, depending on how many characters are in the scene.

3. Using the same idea as above, ask each group to enact the same scene and compare their results. Ask each group to justify the choices made based on textual evidence. You may need to add more actors to each group, depending on how many characters are in the scene.

4. Ask the groups to enact sequential scenes from the novel and see if the story maintains its continuity.

5. Ask the groups to enact the first and last scenes of the novel and discuss what happens to make the characters and situation different at the end than they were at the beginning.

## Collaborating in an Online Environment

With so many components to coordinate, the collaborative process is probably the most challenging to implement remotely. However, with good planning and organization, it can be done, and it is well worth the effort for the learning opportunity it gives the students.

You can orient your students to drama and to the actor's reading process, the designer's reading process, and the director's reading process in a synchronous class session. Utilizing your computer platform's ability, divide the students into three groups, provide each group with their worksheets, and make sure they know what their tasks are. In groups, they can accomplish their respective tasks of searching the text for evidence of character, context, and action, and you can use the platform's ability to move from group to group to coach them and help them formulate their ideas.

When you visit with the group of actors, help them divide up the tasks of creating biographies of the characters, generating the characters' relationships, and filling in any time gaps in the story line. When conferring with the designers, assist them as they work toward envisioning an environment for the story. They can draw sketches of possible design ideas for the environment or use any of a number of simple apps that allow users to create a space and populate it with furniture and characters. Once they have shared their ideas with each other, help them decide on one design for the environment. As you consult with the directors, assist them in finding the story's sequence of actions and remind them that they must envision an environment for the action as well. They can draw sketches of what they envision or use a computer application to render their ideas.

Bring the group of designers and the group of directors together virtually to consult about the arrangement of the environment. Ask them to compare what the designers have created with what the directors have envisioned, consider which ideas best accommodate the story's action, and decide on one design. Your discussion can also include ideas about how to express the story's meaning through the context. Once the designers and directors have agreed on a design, the directors can experiment with action patterns on a computer application, draw arrows on a sketch, or draw a series of sketches.

When the groups have finished their specific tasks, bring them back together in a synchronous class session to integrate all of their ideas. The actors can share their biographies of the characters, talk about the characters' relationships, and inform the class about what happens during any time gaps in the story line. They can also share their ideas about what occurs before the action of the story begins and after it ends. Designers can share their ideas for the environment, and directors can identify the story's action and explain how they would create the action to tell the story.

Engaging your students remotely with the collaborative process will be different from the classroom application. While it will be less of an experiential interaction and more of an interactive discussion, students will still experience the reading process of each artist and see how their work comes together collaboratively.

## Wrap-Up

The collaborative reading process not only gives students specific tasks to accomplish and goals to achieve as they read but also makes them responsible to each other for completing the process. They have certain tasks to accomplish as specific theater artists, yet must integrate their ideas, make decisions collectively, and synthesize information to reach the ultimate goal. The process also develops students' higher-order reading and thinking skills by challenging them to identify and combine multiple layers of meaning in a text. Partnering with both the text and each other, students are challenged by the collaborative reading process to explore text from different perspectives and work together in the meaning-making process.

## A Concluding Word on the Reading Strategies

As teachers, we all want our students to be good readers. We want them to love reading as much as we do. Some students are naturals at it. They read easily and create mental pictures and images as they read. But others aren't so lucky. They don't see or envision what they read, and consequently they find reading to be a dull and tedious task they must wade through. These students are not dumb or lazy; they need reading strategies that teach them how to see beyond the printed text to find the world it evokes.

The strategies in this book are meant to do just that. They serve as training tools to assist readers and scaffolds to help them interact with text to uncover evidence, ask questions, and envision the characters, context, and action of a story. The actor's process, the designer's process, the director's process, and the collaborative process give readers specific ways to interact with text, build on what the writer has provided, and transform reading into the adventure and experience it is meant to be. Learning these skills and becoming more proficient readers, however, requires practice. We don't learn or perfect a skill by doing it once. I hope you will not only teach your students these reading strategies but also encourage them to continue to practice them as they read, both in and out of the classroom. The more they practice and apply the skills of reading as actors, designers, and directors, the more comprehensively they will understand the characters, contexts, and actions they encounter in literature.

Theater artists continually practice. An accomplished actor, designer, or director is repeatedly interacting with text, envisioning it, and bringing its life and meaning to the stage. The more they do it, the better they become at it, and ultimately, without even thinking about the process, they see the stage picture as they read. Over time, the same will happen for student readers, who will no longer need to consciously build characters' lives, construct a story's context, or enact its action in the classroom. Instead, they will convert these skills to mental interaction every time they read. It will not happen overnight; it will happen with practice. An old theater story tells of a young man who encounters an old man on the streets of New York. "How do I get to Carnegie Hall?" asks the young man. "Practice, my son," replies the old man. "Practice."

# Additional Classroom Drama Strategies

In addition to the specific reading strategies outlined in this book, there are many other ways to integrate drama into your classroom. This section gives you a specific strategy for engaging students with dramatic literature and briefly describes some of the most popular drama strategies you can use to help students interact with all literary work.

# A Production Team Approach to Studying Dramatic Literature

# 9

## Why This Approach to Dramatic Literature?

Dramatic literature is generally included in the English language arts curriculum, yet often teachers are unsure how to approach it. Indeed, because dramatic literature is written to be transformed into production, it often falls flat when studied exclusively as written literature. This chapter explains a learning strategy you can use to engage readers in the study of dramatic literature by providing them with an opportunity to examine a play as both literature and production.

This strategy positions students as actors, designers, and directors working together as a production team to plan and justify the production of a play. It models Dorothy Heathcote's mantle of the expert approach, utilizing the creation of an imaginary classroom enterprise in which students are not just receivers of information but servicers of it as they work toward specific goals. The objective of each production team is to develop and organize a presentation to convince a group of investors—the rest of the class—to provide financial support for their production. Thus, as students listen to each other's presentations, they also assume the role of potential financial investors, considering whether they will support the productions that other teams present.

The strategy also incorporates the teacher-in-role as a producer, coaching each group of students toward their goals and modeling the steps of the process. As producer, you can decide how far to take this fictional enterprise. You may want to allow the investors in the audience to ask questions of each production team, or you may not want to take the time. It is completely up to you. Either way, involving the students as audience members as well as presenters keeps them engaged and offers them an additional perspective on the literature.

The production team approach is a strategy that requires students to think beyond what is on the page and work independently as well as collaboratively. It may not be appropriate for all students. If you find the project too complex, think about using parts of it for your students' study of dramatic literature. The time frame for this project is variable; it can be accomplished in a week if your students are good independent readers and workers, or it can take longer if your students need more time for reading and preparation.

## Introducing the Strategy

To successfully participate in this approach to dramatic literature, students must know the basic responsibilities of theater artists and how they work together to create a production. If you have introduced your students to the processes of reading as an actor, reading as a designer, reading as a director, and reading collaboratively, you have already accomplished the front-loading for this project. If they are unfamiliar with these concepts, you will need to provide some basic background. Reviewing Section I, Reading as a Theater Artist, will provide the information you need. I begin the project by giving students the following introductory information:

> We will be studying a piece of dramatic literature, _____name of the play_____ by _____playwright_____. Although it is a written text, dramatic literature is designed to be translated into action for the stage, so we will focus our study toward both the written text and its production. The class will be divided into small groups to form production teams, each made up of actors, designers, and directors. Once you are assigned to your production team, you may decide who functions in which roles within your group.
>
> As a production team, you have the job of generating a vision for a theatrical presentation of the play. As a group, you will create a fifteen-minute oral presentation to a group of investors, convincing them to provide funding and support for your production. The investors will be hearing multiple requests and can support only one production, so you must persuade them that **yours** is the one they should choose. Although your presentation is oral, you will submit a written version of it so that the investors can also see your concepts in writing.
>
> Each team will receive specific written instructions describing its tasks.

## Size of Production Teams

Ideally, you will divide your class into groups of three to accomplish this project, with each group having one actor, one designer, and one director. For a class of thirty-six, however, this approach would create twelve groups, which would probably take way too much time when you get to the presentation stage. If instead you place six students in each group, you can designate two actors, two designers, and two directors who can share the tasks of each type of artist. This approach creates six presentation groups, which is probably more manageable over two presentation days. Try to avoid groups larger than six, as they will not function as efficiently. Ultimately, use your judgment in deciding how to divide your class to apply this strategy in the best way for your students, the dramatic literature you are using, and the time you wish to allot to the project.

## Engaging Your Librarian

To help students with the research they need to do for this project, I usually set up a session with the school librarian to inform students about the resources and databases available to them and how to use them. I share the project with the librarian ahead of time and explain it so that the librarian knows what the students are looking for and can help guide them to appropriate resources. If you don't have the luxury of a school librarian, you will probably need to assist your students with this information.

## Instructions for the Presentation

After providing the introductory information, I give students the following written instructions for their presentation, detailing their responsibilities both as a production team and as individuals within a team. Their responsibilities include completing a worksheet for each individual and a work calendar for the whole group. You will find the individual worksheets in this section and the work calendar in the section on time management; they are also included as individual handouts in the appendix. Feel free to use them, modify them, or, of course, create our own.

### Your Presentation to the Investors

**Responsibilities of the Whole Team**

1. Introduction: Give yourselves a good strong introduction that captures the interest of the audience. The investors do not know anything about you, your play, or how a production team works. Each member of your team must give a self-introduction and explain their job and what their part of the production entails.

2. Conclusion: Conclude your presentation in a way that summarizes the importance of your ideas, leaves the investors with a positive impression, and gives them a reason to want to provide funding for *your* production.

3. Submit your completed written work calendar.

**Responsibilities of the Actor**

1. Present an oral and written summary of the plot, as well as a short description of each character, including discussion of how each character is important to the play.

2. Present an oral and written biography for one character from the play.

3. Submit your completed written worksheet.

**Responsibilities of the Designer**

1. Create, present, and explain a visual collage depicting the main imagery of the play.

2. Create, present, and explain at least one drawing of the space(s) needed for presentation of the play. Describe what in the play's context needs to be included to accommodate the action of the story and how the environment you create will help reflect the meaning of the play.

3. If the designer wishes, costume drawings can be included as well, but they are not required.

4. Submit your completed written worksheet.

**Responsibilities of the Director**

1. Present an oral and written description of the sequence of actions in the play from beginning to end.

2. Present an oral and written summary of the social and historical context of the play, including why it was significant when it was written and why it is an important play for today's audience.

3. Present an oral and written summary of the background of the playwright, including what else this playwright has written and why this writer is an important voice for today's audience.

4. Submit your completed written worksheet.

• • • • • • • • •

## Production Team Worksheet for the Actor

1. What is my job in the production of the play, and what do I need to know from the directors and the designers?

2. Who are the characters in the play? Why is each one in the story?

3. How do the characters relate to each other?

4. What are the characters' backgrounds?

5. What events in the characters' lives have occurred right before the play begins? Give two examples of how the playwright's word choice tells you something about the characters.

6. How do the characters change over the course of the play, and what happens to cause those changes?

* * * * * * * * * *

## Production Team Worksheet for the Designer

1. What is my job in the production of the play, and what do I need to know from the directors and the actors?

2. What is the play's context?

3. What does the environment need to include in order to accommodate the story's action?

4. Is there only one location, or does the story move around?

5. Give two examples of how the playwright's word choice tells you something about the environment.

6. What year is it? Season? Time of day?

7. How much time elapses during the story?

8. What colors, textures, shapes, and images reflect the play's meaning and significance?

* * * * * * * * * *

**Production Team Worksheet for the Director**

1. What is my job in the production of the play, and what do I need to know from the designers and the actors?

2. What sequence of physical action tells the story of the play?

3. How does the dialogue or verbal action tell the story of the play?

4. Give two examples of how the playwright's word choice tells you something about the action.

5. Who is the playwright, and why did the playwright choose to tell this story?

6. Does the story relate to the playwright's life? If so, how?

7. What was the significance of the play to its original audience?

8. What is the significance of the play to today's audience?

9. Why is it important to present this play?

## Time Management

You will need to determine how much time to allocate for this project. If you have students who are motivated, quick readers, and you are using a short one-act play, you can probably accomplish the tasks of this project in a week. If your students need more reading time, or if you are using a full-length play, you will likely need additional time. You can use the whole project or just select parts of it that might work for you. I have used it as a four-week project with community college students, a full-length play, and the optional components.

When students engage in this project, they must manage their time so that all components are completed by the deadline. As they do this, they are essentially creating a rehearsal schedule for themselves. Often, the idea of planning out a work schedule is unfamiliar to students, so I guide them (as producer) through the steps of this process. When they begin the project, I help them determine what work they are responsible for each day, ensuring that all tasks are accounted for and finished by the deadline. A sample time management worksheet is provided in Figure 9.1 and also appears in the book's appendix. You may use this worksheet as is or modify it to accommodate your work schedule for this project. Alternatively, I sometimes give students a blank calendar starting with the date on which the project begins and ending with the date of their presentation. I ask them to fill in what work is due on each day and make sure all tasks are accounted for on time.

| Monday | Tuesday | Wednesday | Thursday | Friday |
|--------|---------|-----------|----------|--------|
| **All:** Select production roles. Review job of each team member. Make work assignments. Agree on production calendar. Everyone read the play by tomorrow! | **All:** **Library research.** **Actor:** Detail plot of the play. Analyze characters' importance to today's audience. Write character biography. **Designer:** Determine spaces that are needed and how to represent them. Create preliminary sketch. Create collage. **Director:** Determine sequence of the play's action. Research time era and production history of the play. Research playwright. | **All:** **Share research.** **Actor:** Share plot summary. Share characters' relevance to today. Share biography. Accept feedback. **Designer:** Share sketch of space—consult with director as to whether it will accommodate the play's action. Share how the environment reflects the play's meaning. Share collage. Accept feedback. **Director:** Share sequence of the story's actions. Consult with designer concerning space and action. Share significance of time era and relevance to today's audience. Share information on playwright. Accept feedback. | **All:** **Dress rehearsal.** **All:** Create and practice introduction. **Actor:** Present plot summary and why story is important today. Present biography. Report on status of written portion. **Designer:** Present sketch and collage and describe significance of each. Define significance of setting to the play's meaning. Report on status of written portion. **Director** Present social and historical context of the play and relevance to today's audience. Present info on playwright and play's message. Report on status of written portion. **All:** Create and practice conclusion. | **All:** Make oral presentation. Hand in written component. |

**FIGURE 9.1.** Example of a time management worksheet for the team.

## Optional Components

These elements of the project require additional preparation time. Your decision to include any or all of them will be determined by the level of your students and the amount of time you want to devote to this project. Any or all of these components can also be used as individual assignments in the study of dramatic literature.

1. Create a publicity poster for your production. Decide what visual image will best represent and sell your production and incorporate it into a promotional poster.

2. Select and present a short scene from your play that demonstrates the play's significance. You will need to construct a simple representation of the environment and enact the scene's action within it. Introduce your scene with appropriate background so the audience can understand the action. Select and provide appropriate music to begin and end your scene.

3. Create an educational outreach plan for your production. What specific groups would you target as an audience for this production, why, and how would you promote the production to them?

Any of these optional components can also be used as individual assignments in the study of dramatic literature.

## Adapting This Strategy to Other Literary Genres

The basic idea of this strategy is that you are creating an imaginary enterprise in the classroom, giving students the mantle of a particular expert, and asking them to use knowledge as source material to create a product for a client. With a little creativity, you can adapt this project to other literary genres, and any of the following suggestions can be implemented as either individual or group assignments. Feel free to use any of these ideas, modify them, or create your own projects.

1. Assume the role of an author or coauthors of a short story. Justify the inclusion of your story in a printed anthology. Explain what is significant about this story to a group of editors and rationalize why it should be included in an anthology for today's readers. You can use a published short story or one written by a student.

2. Assume the role of an author or coauthors of a novel. Justify the publication of the novel to an editor. Convince the editor that the message of the novel is important for today's readers. You can use a novel you have studied in class.

3. Assume the role of a Broadway producer or group of producers. Justify to a group of financial advisors the value of transforming a particular novel into a stage production.

4. Assume the role of a movie producer or group of producers. Convince a group of financial investors to support your plan to make a movie adaptation of a novel. Explain why the novel is important and how it will be adapted into a film.

5. Assume the role of a struggling poet. Convince an editor to publish your poem so you can make some money to buy food. Justify the value of your poem for a contemporary audience. Use a published poem or one written by a student.

## The Production Team Approach Online

This approach to dramatic literature, which serves both its literary and its production aspects, makes for a complex project. Although it can be implemented in an online environment, doing so may be challenging. If you have the time and resources, you can implement the project online basically as it is described. You can orient students to this new strategy in a synchronous online session and then, using your computer platform's ability to break students into smaller groups, let them work in groups as production teams. Students can then make their presentations to each other via Zoom or another video teleconferencing application. Although you will visit and coach each group virtually in your role as producer, the project will require a great deal of independent work and self-motivation on the part of your students.

You can also consider using only parts of the whole project as an online option. Any of the responsibilities of the actor, designer, or director can be used as a single assignment on which students can work individually or collaboratively. Think creatively about how you can adapt this project to your students and the dramatic literature you use as part of your curriculum.

## Wrap-Up

This is a challenging project for highly motivated and self-disciplined students. It requires them to work on their own as well as collaboratively. You might want to start by implementing part of the project and work up to engaging your students with the whole thing. Since it involves working to a hard deadline, it is an excellent way to teach students time management skills. Just as they would if they were participating in a rehearsal process for a stage production, they must complete all of their tasks to be ready for "opening night."

# 10 Other Interactive Approaches to Engage Students with Text

The techniques presented here for integrating drama into your classroom can be adapted to any type of literature and used with other teaching strategies. You can implement the ideas as described, modify them to meet the needs of your students or a particular piece of literature, or, of course, create your own.

Try to implement these strategies in ways that give everyone a chance to participate, so that active engagement is not limited to those who jump in quickly. It may take some students more time and encouragement than others to warm up to interactive activities. As you use these activities, try to find ways to participate in role. Students are often more willing to engage if you are participating too, and doing so puts you in a position to control the activities, maintain the focus you want, and keep students on task.

## Role-Playing, or Enactment

Role-playing, or enactment, involves readers using their bodies and voices to physicalize and vocalize characters, actions, or ideas. Characters can be drawn from literature or history or created from the imagination.

### How Can You Use It in Your Classroom?

1. Students assume the roles of characters in a story and enact the whole story or parts of it.

2. Different students enact the same story, then discuss or write about how their interpretations differed and why.

3. Groups of students enact sequential parts of a story, then discuss or write about how actions interconnect.

4. Students improvise actions by a story's characters in circumstances other than those presented in the story. How would the characters behave and

why? Students then discuss or write about what the text tells them about characters that would influence how they behave in different circumstances.

5. Students create characters who are not in a story and have them talk to the story's characters.

6. Students write a story that integrates characters from a literary text with characters they create.

7. Students enact characters from history to make presentations to the class about life in another era.

8. Students enact various characters from history to talk with each other. What would they talk about?

# Tableau

A tableau (singular) is a still physical representation similar to a statue. It can be a representation of a person, a concept, or a moment in a story. Students can build tableaux (plural) with their bodies to explain or describe something as an alternative to speech or writing and to help make abstract ideas more concrete.

## How Can You Use It in Your Classroom?

1. Students can express the meaning of a vocabulary word with their bodies.

2. Tableaux can be used to help illuminate the meaning of a concept or idea from literature. A group of students can work together to create a tableau of an abstract concept such as intolerance. What does intolerance look like?

3. Have different groups of students create statues of intolerance. Compare. How are they similar? How are they different? Are there different kinds of intolerance? Are there different interpretations of intolerance?

4. Looking at one of the statues, ask a student to change it from intolerance to tolerance. How can intolerance be changed into tolerance? This activity can be done with any abstract concept.

5. Ask a group of students to create a tableau of a specific incident or event in a story. If you could freeze a moment of the story, what would it look like?

6. Divide the class into groups and assign each group a part of a story or novel. Ask each group to create a tableau that represents the essence of that part.

7. Ask students to create tableaux of parts of a published story or one they have written and then arrange them to reflect the sequence of events in the story.

8. Look at tableaux that follow the flow of the story. Discuss what happens to change the story from one tableau to the next.

9. Clarifying important points in a story: Ask students to define the three most important points in a story and create a tableau that represents each one. Discuss what happens to change the story from tableau one to tableau two to tableau three.

10. Moving tableaux: Ask a student or group of students to create a tableau of a moment in a story and show how that point in the story transforms into what happens next.

## Hot Seat

With this technique, students assume a role and act as someone or something other than themselves. As they "sit in the hot seat," they must carry on a conversation and answer questions in the role of the person (or concept) they assume.

### How Can You Use It in Your Classroom?

Any of the hot-seat activities can be done as extemporaneous improvisations where students have to think quickly on the spot, or you can give students time to prepare for these conversations in more depth.

1. **Talk show:** Designate students as the characters in a story and ask them all to appear as guests on a talk show. You can act as the host and ask them questions or allow members of the audience (the rest of the class) to ask questions. You can limit questions to events that occur in the story or ask those in the hot seat to extrapolate and go beyond the story. If you participate in role as the talk show host, you can focus the discussion and keep it from getting off track.

2. **Intertextuality:** Have characters from different stories sit in the hot seat, talk to each other, and ask each other questions.

3. **Historical characters:** Ask students to sit in the hot seat as characters from history and talk to each other and answer questions.

4. **Clarifying concepts:** Ask students to sit in the hot seat as an idea or concept and answer questions about what they represent.

## Good Angel/Bad Angel/Subtext

This is a technique you can use by itself or in conjunction with the hot seat. Someone enacts a character or idea, and a "good angel" and a "bad angel" sit on either side of the character and give advice regarding an important decision. The angels act as the character's subtext, verbalizing what the character is thinking before making a decision.

### How Can You Use It in Your Classroom?

1. Designate a student to assume the role of a character who has to make an important decision. Place a student on either side of the character. Have the good angel speak to the character as their conscience, to convince them to make a positive decision, and have the bad angel advocate a negative decision. Have the character listen to both angels, weigh the evidence, and make a decision.

2. Enact a portion of a story. Assign a good angel and a bad angel for each character and have the angels speak to the characters as the action flows. This device makes visible what the character is thinking before speaking.

3. Have a good angel and a bad angel advise a character on the pros and cons of a course of action before making a crucial decision.


## Mantle of the Expert

You already know this strategy from the chapters in Section I, Reading as a Theater Artist, but there are additional ways to apply this strategy in your classroom. Asking students to assume the mantle or responsibility of another person and step into their shoes repositions them as readers and writers and gives them the opportunity to view a piece of literature or a subject from another perspective.

### How Can You Use It in Your Classroom?

1. Determine the theme of a piece of literature and ask students to discuss or write about the story from the point of view of an expert in a relevant field.

2. Ask students to assume the role of a filmmaker to discuss or write about how they would make a film from a given novel.

3. Ask students to assume the mantle of a doctor, lawyer, scientist, or social worker and discuss the issues faced by characters in a story or novel from the perspective of those professionals.

## Teacher-in-Role

In this approach, you assume a role other than that of teacher. You have already done this as you've guided students through reading as an actor, reading as a designer, reading as a director, and reading collaboratively. Here are some other ways you can engage with students in role.

### How Can You Use It in Your Classroom?

1. **Hot-seating:** You can sit in the hot seat, assume the role of a character from a story, and allow students to ask you questions. You may be able to explain concepts more clearly as the character than as the teacher.
2. **Guest Appearance:** You can assume the role of an expert in a certain field related to the literature you are studying. Allow students to ask the expert questions about the literature.
3. **You Know Nothing:** Assume the role of someone who knows nothing about a certain piece of literature or concept. Ask the students explain it to you. Ask them questions about it.

## Writing in Role

Instead of writing as themselves, students write assuming the persona of another person or a character from a story. This activity challenges students to write from a different perspective.

### How Can You Use It in Your Classroom?

1. **As an expert:** Ask students to write about a topic as an expert in the field.
2. **As characters from a story:** Ask students to write letters to each other as characters from a story.
3. **Intertextually:** Have characters from different stories write to each other.

4.  **As historical characters:** Have historical characters write letters to today's students.

For a more detailed account of many of these strategies, please see Wilhelm's *Deepening Comprehension with Action Strategies: Role Plays, Text-Structure Tableaux, Talking Statues, and Other Enactment Techniques That Engage Students with Text*.

## Using These Strategies in an Online Environment

While most of these additional drama strategies for engaging students with text are best used in a physical classroom, they can be adapted to remote learning as well. Individually, students can write about or draw how they would enact a particular story or build a tableau to represent a part of a story or a concept. They can also imagine themselves as a literary character in the hot seat and create questions for the character to answer, and they can discuss or write about what a good angel or a bad angel might whisper to them if they were a character in a story who had to make a major decision. Mantle of the expert, hot seat, and good/bad angel can also be used with computer applications that allow students to see and talk with each other.

In addition, you can create written assignments where students write in role as either a literary or a historical character, giving them the opportunity to write from the perspective of someone else. You can also combine writing in role with the mantle of the expert approach by having students write from the point of view of someone who is an expert in a given field. An example would be having students write about a mentally challenged literary character from the point of view of a psychiatrist.

Finally, you can always find ways to interact with your students in role, asking them questions or coaching them through assignments as someone other than yourself. Think creatively as you read these strategies and find innovative ways to adapt them to a remote teaching environment.

## Wrap-Up

All of these additional drama strategies that actively engage students with text reorient readers from receiving information to constructing knowledge, making them active agents in the reading process. As students participate in these activities, they interact with text and see it from multiple perspectives, building on what the writer has supplied to find meaning. Drama, in all its forms, creates a generative and dynamic learning environment that facilitates the understanding of text, makes it concrete and meaningful, and transforms reading into a process of continual discovery.

# Appendix

*Worksheets*

---

### The Actor's Worklist

**A.** Search for and record evidence of character from the text.

    **1.** What is the full name of each character in the text?

    **2.** What does the text explicitly tell you about each character?

    **3.** What is the age, date of birth, and place of birth of each character?

    **4.** Where do the characters live?

    **5.** What are the important traits of each character?

    **6.** What are the relationships between the characters at the beginning of the text?

    **7.** What are the relationships of the characters at the end of the text?

    **8.** What happens to make the characters different by the end of the text?

    **9.** Are there any time gaps in the story line?

**B.** Combine the character evidence you have found in the text with your own imagination to write a biography of each character.

**C.** Combine the character evidence you have found in the text with your own imagination to write about the characters' relationships.

**D.** Combine the character evidence you have found in the text with your own imagination to fill in any time gaps in the story line.

**Searching the Text for Evidence of Character**

**Literary work title:**

1. What is the full name of each character in the story?

2. What does the text explicitly tell you about each character?

3. What is the age, date of birth, and place of birth of each character?

4. Where do the characters live?

5. What are the important traits of each character?

6. What are the relationships between the characters at the beginning of the text?

7. What are the relationships between the characters at the end of the text?

8. What happens to make the characters different by the end of the text?

9. Identify any time gaps in the story line.

## Actor's Character Biography Worksheet

Literary work title:

Actor(s):

Character biography of:

| | |
|---|---|
| Date and place of birth / age in story | |
| Parents | |
| Siblings | |
| Childhood memories | |
| Education | |
| Work history | |
| Important relationships | |
| Significant life events | |

## Actor's Character Relationship Worksheet

Literary work:

Actor(s):

| Characters | Present relationship | Past relationship | Relationship change in the story |
|---|---|---|---|
|  |  |  |  |
|  |  |  |  |
|  |  |  |  |
|  |  |  |  |
|  |  |  |  |

## Actor's Worksheet for Any Time Gaps in the Story Line

Literary work title:

Actor(s):

| Time gap | Amount of time | What happens |
|---|---|---|
|  |  |  |
|  |  |  |
|  |  |  |
|  |  |  |
| Time before the story begins |  |  |
| Time after the story ends |  |  |

## The Designer's Worklist

**A.** Search the text to find and record the following information:

    **1.** Where does the action take place? Does it occur in more than one location?

    **2.** If characters move from one location to another, what are the requirements, if any, for space between the locations?

    **3.** What is the time period? Past? Present? Future?

    **4.** At what time(s) of day does the action occur?

    **5.** What is the season?

    **6.** How can our classroom be rearranged to represent the location(s) of the text?

    **7.** What does the environment need to include (e.g., walkways, walls, doors, windows, stairways, furniture, props) to accommodate the action of the text?

**B.** Using the available space and furniture, visualize the text's environment in the classroom.

**C.** Determine how the environment will accommodate the action of the text.

**D.** Draw a sketch of how you envision reconfiguring the classroom to create the text's environment.

**E.** Create a representation of the context in the classroom.

## Searching the Text for Evidence of Context

**Literary work title:**

1. Where does the action take place? Does it occur in more than one location?

2. If characters move from one location to another, what are the requirements, if any, for space between the locations?

3. What is the time period? Past? Present? Future?

4. At what time(s) of day does the action occur?

5. What is the season?

6. How can our classroom be rearranged to represent the location(s) of the text?

7. What does the environment need to include (e.g., walkways, walls, doors, windows, stairways, furniture, props) to accommodate the action of the text?

## Designer's Context Worksheet

Literary work title:

Set designer(s):

| | |
|---|---|
| Number of locations | |
| Location definition(s) | |
| Time era references | |
| Time(s) of day or night | |
| Season(s) | |
| Reflection of characters in the environment | |

## Designer's Space Worksheet

Literary work title:

Set designer(s):

| Space we need | How can we use the classroom and its objects to create this space? |
|---|---|
|  |  |
|  |  |
|  |  |

## Designer's Prop Worksheet

Literary work title:

Set designer(s):

| Props we need | Who brings in |
|---|---|
|  |  |
|  |  |
|  |  |
|  |  |
|  |  |
|  |  |

## Designer's Action Worksheet

Literary work title:

Set designer(s):

| Important action in the story | Arrangement of the set to accommodate it |
|---|---|
|  |  |
|  |  |
|  |  |
|  |  |

## The Director's Worklist

**A.** Identify the sequence of physical and verbal actions that tell the story from beginning to end.

    **1.** What is the sequence of actions that takes the characters from the beginning of the text to the end? (Look specifically for action verbs and <u>underline</u> them).

    **2.** Revisit your list of actions, this time from the last action to the first. Has each action has been motivated by the previous one, thus verifying the continuity of the text?

    **3.** What does each character's voice sound like?

    **4.** What is happening during any pauses?

**B.** How can our classroom be rearranged to represent the location(s) of the text? What needs to be in the environment to accommodate the action of the text? What furniture and props are needed? Sketch out a rough drawing of the environment.

**C.** Construct the environment in the classroom and transform the action into concrete reality in the environment.

## Searching the Text for Evidence of Action

**Literary work title:**

1. What is the sequence of actions that takes the characters from the beginning of the text to the end? (Look specifically for action verbs and <u>underline</u> them.)

2. Revisit your list of actions, this time from the last action to the first. Has each action been motivated by the previous one, thus verifying the continuity of the text?

3. What does each character's voice sound like?

4. Determine what is happening during any pauses.

## Director's Action Worksheet

Literary work title:

Director(s):

Character:

| Physical action | Verbal action |
|-----------------|---------------|
|                 |               |
|                 |               |
|                 |               |
|                 |               |
|                 |               |
|                 |               |
|                 |               |
|                 |               |
|                 |               |
|                 |               |
|                 |               |

**Production Team Worksheet for the Actor**

1. What is my job relating to the production of the play and what do I need to know from the director and the designer?

2. Who are the characters? Why is each one in the text?

3. How do the characters relate to each other?

4. What are the characters' backgrounds?

5. What events in the characters' lives have occurred right before the play begins?

6. Give two examples of how the playwright's word choice tells you something about the characters.

7. How do the characters change over the course of the play and what happens to cause those changes?

## Production Team Worksheet for the Designer

1.  What is my job relating to the production of the play and what do I need to know from the director and the actors?

2.  What is the play's context?

3.  What does the environment need to include to accommodate the story's action?

4.  Is there one location or does the story move to different locations?

5.  Give two examples of how the playwright's word choice tells you something about the environment.

6.  What year is it? Season? Time of Day?

7.  How much time elapses during the story?

8.  What colors, textures, shapes, and images reflect the play's meaning and significance?

**Production Team Worksheet for the Director**

1. What is my job relating to the production of the play and what do I need to know from the designer and the actors?

2. What is the sequence of physical action that tells the story of the play?

3. How does the dialogue or verbal action tell the story of the play?

4. Give two examples of how the playwright's word choice tells you something about the action.

5. Who is the playwright and why did he or she choose to tell this story?

6. Does the story relate to the playwright's life?

7. What was the significance of the play to its original audience?

8. What is its significance of the play to today's audience?

9. Why is it important to present this play?

| Monday | Tuesday | Wednesday | Thursday | Friday |
|---|---|---|---|---|
| **All:**<br><br>Select production roles.<br><br>Review job of each team member.<br><br>Make work assignments.<br><br>Agree on production calendar.<br><br>Everyone read the play by tomorrow! | **All:**<br>**Library research.**<br><br>**Actor:**<br>Detail plot of the play.<br>Analyze characters' importance to today's audience.<br>Write character biography.<br><br>**Designer:**<br>Determine spaces that are needed and how to represent them.<br>Create preliminary sketch.<br>Create collage.<br><br>**Director:**<br>Determine sequence of the play's action.<br>Research time era and production history of the play.<br>Research playwright. | **All:**<br>**Share research.**<br><br>**Actor:**<br>Share plot summary.<br>Share characters' relevance to today.<br>Share biography.<br>Accept feedback.<br><br>**Designer:**<br>Share sketch of space—consult with director as to whether it will accommodate the play's action.<br>Share how the environment reflects the play's meaning.<br>Share collage.<br>Accept feedback.<br><br>**Director:**<br>Share sequence of the story's actions. Consult with designer concerning space and action.<br>Share significance of time era and relevance to today's audience.<br> Share information on playwright.<br>Accept feedback. | **All:**<br>**Dress rehearsal.**<br><br>**All:**<br>Create and practice introduction.<br><br>**Actor:**<br>Present plot summary and why story is important today.<br>Present biography. Report on status of written portion.<br><br>**Designer:**<br>Present sketch and collage and describe significance of each. Define significance of setting to the play's meaning.<br>Report on status of written portion.<br><br>**Director**<br>Present social and historical context of the play and relevance to today's audience.<br>Present info on playwright and play's message.<br>Report on status of written portion.<br>**All:**<br>Create and practice conclusion. | **All:**<br><br>Make oral presentation.<br>Hand in written component. |

# References

Arnold, Stephanie. *The Creative Spirit*. Mayfield, 2001.

Ball, David. *Backwards and Forwards: A Technical Manual for Reading Plays*. Southern Illinois UP, 1983.

Benedetti, Robert. *The Actor in You: Sixteen Simple Steps to Understanding the Art of Acting*. Allyn & Bacon, 2012.

Boal, Augusto. *Games for Actors and Non-Actors*. Routledge, 1992.

Bolton, Gavin, and Dorothy Heathcote. *So You Want to Use Role Play? A New Approach in How to Plan*. Trentham, 1999.

Bowell, Pamela, and Brian S. Heap. *Planning Process Drama*. Routledge, 2013.

Bruner, Jerome. *Acts of Meaning*. Harvard UP, 1990.

Bruner, Jerome. *Actual Minds, Possible Worlds*. Harvard UP, 1986.

Cohen, Robert. *Theater*. Mayfield, 1997.

Cole, David. *Acting as Reading*. U of Michigan P, 1992.

Courtney, Richard. *Play, Drama and Thought: The Intellectual Background to Drama in Education*. Drama Book Specialists, 1968.

Cross, K. Patricia, and Mimi Harris Steadman. *Classroom Research: Implementing the Scholarship of Teaching*. Jossey-Bass, 1996.

Davis, David, editor. *Interactive Research in Drama in Education*. Trentham, 1997.

Davis, Susan, et al., editors. *Dramatic Interactions in Education: Vygotskian and Sociocultural Approaches to Drama, Education and Research*. Bloomsbury, 2016.

Dawson, Kathryn, and Bridget Kiger Lee. *Drama-Based Pedagogy: Activating Learning Across the Curriculum*. U of Chicago P, 2018.

Dean, Alexander, and Lawrence Carra. *Fundamentals of Play Directing*. Waveland Press, 1989.

Dewey, John. *Experience and Education*. Touchstone, 1938.

Dixon, John. *Growth through English: A Report Based on the Dartmouth Seminar 1966*. Oxford UP, 1967.

Edmiston, Brian. *Transforming Teaching and Learning with Active and Dramatic Approaches: Engaging Students Across the Curriculum.* Routledge, 2014.

Elbow. Peter. *What Is English?* Modern Language Association of America, 1990.

Gardner, Howard. *Frames of Mind: The Theory of Multiple Intelligences.* Basic Books, 1983.

Gillette, J. Michael. *Theatrical Design and Production.* McGraw Hill, 2013.

Heathcote, Dorothy. *Collected Writings on Education and Drama.* Northwestern UP, 1991.

Heathcote, Dorothy, and Gavin Bolton. *Drama for Learning: Dorothy Heathcote's Mantle of the Expert Approach to Education.* Heinemann, 1995.

Hornbrook, David. *Education and Dramatic Art.* Routledge, 1998.

Jones, Robert Edmond. *The Dramatic Imagination.* Routledge, 1969.

Kelner, Lenore Blank, and Rosalind M. Flynn. *A Dramatic Approach to Reading Comprehension: Strategies and Activities for Classroom Teachers.* Heinemann, 2006.

Landy, Robert J. *Handbook of Educational Drama and Theater.* Greenwood Press, 1982.

Moffett, James. *Teaching the Universe of Discourse.* Houghton Mifflin, 1968.

Moffett, James, and Betty Jane Wagner. *Student-Centered Language Arts and Reading K–13.* Houghton Mifflin, 1976.

Moore, Sonia. *The Stanislavski System.* Penguin, 1984.

Muller, Herbert J. *The Uses of English: Guidelines for the Teaching English from the Anglo-American Conference at Dartmouth College.* Holt, Rinehart and Winston, 1967.

National Governors Association Center for Best Practices and Council of Chief State School Officers. *Common Core State Standards Initiative.* "Common Core State Standards for English Language Arts & Literacy in History/Social Studies, Science, and Technical Subjects," 2010, corestandards.org/ELA-Literacy/.

O'Neill, Cecily, editor. *Dorothy Heathcote on Education and Drama: Essential Writings.* Routledge, 2015.

O'Neill, Cecily. *Drama Worlds: A Framework for Process Drama.* Heinemann, 1995.

Rosenblatt, Louise M. *Literature as Exploration.* 1938. 4th ed., Modern Language Association of America, 1983.

Smith, Michael, and Jeffrey D. Wilhelm. *"Reading Don't Fix No Chevys": Literacy in the Lives of Young Men.* Heinemann, 2002.

Stanislavski, Constantin. *An Actor Prepares.* Routledge, 1988.

van de Water, Manon, et al. *Drama and Education: Performance Methodologies for Teaching and Learning.* Routledge, 2015.

Vygotsky, L.S. *Mind in Society: The Development of Higher Psychological Processes.* Harvard UP, 1978.

Wagner, Betty Jane. *Dorothy Heathcote: Drama as a Learning Medium.* National Education Association, 1976.

Wagner, Betty Jane. *Educational Drama and Language Arts: What Research Shows*. Heinemann, 1998.

Wertsch, James V. *Vygotsky and the Social Formation of Mind*. Harvard UP, 1985.

Whitmore, Kathryn F., et al. "Drama-Based Literacies." *Position Statements*. National Council of Teachers of English, 5 Aug. 2020, https://ncte.org/statement/drama-based-literacies/.

Wilhelm, Jeffrey D. *Deepening Comprehension with Action Strategies: Role Plays, Text-Structure Tableaux, Talking Statues, and Other Enactment Techniques That Engage Students with Text*. Scholastic, 2012.

Wilhelm, Jeffrey D. *"You Gotta BE the Book": Teaching Engaged and Reflective Reading with Adolescents*. Teachers College Press, 1997.

Wilhelm, Jeffrey D., and Brian Edmiston. *Imagining to Learn: Inquiry, Ethics, and Integration through Drama*. Heinemann, 1998.

Wilson, Edwin. *The Theater Experience*. McGraw Hill, 2011.

# Index

# Author

Retired theater professor **Judith Freeman Garey** taught in the California Community College system for more than thirty-five years, serving as department chair for theater and dance at Ventura College for many years. In addition to her recognition as an outstanding stage director by the Kennedy Center American College Theater Festival, she is a national scholar with the Carnegie Academy for the Scholarship of Teaching and Learning and a fellow of the South Coast Writing Project. Her article "Activating Reading: Giving Readers the Tools to See and Hear What They Read" appeared in the journal *California English* in November 2016. She holds an MA in theater from the University of Illinois and a PhD in education from the University of California, Santa Barbara.

This book was typeset in TheMix and Palatino by Barbara Frazier.

Typefaces used on the cover include Eveleth and Avenir Next.

The book was printed on 50-lb. White Offset paper by Seaway Printing Company, Inc.